THE EXCELLENCY OF THE
ENGLISH TONGUE

THE EXCELLENCY OF
THE ENGLISH TONGUE

F. E. Halliday

LONDON
VICTOR GOLLANCZ LTD
1975

ISBN 0 575 02020 2

Printed in Great Britain
by Ebenezer Baylis and Son Limited
The Trinity Press, Worcester, and London

for
CALLUM

ACKNOWLEDGMENT

The author thanks Sir John Summerson and Mr George Wingfield Digby for helping him to obtain some of the illustrations in this book

CONTENTS

ILLUSTRATIONS

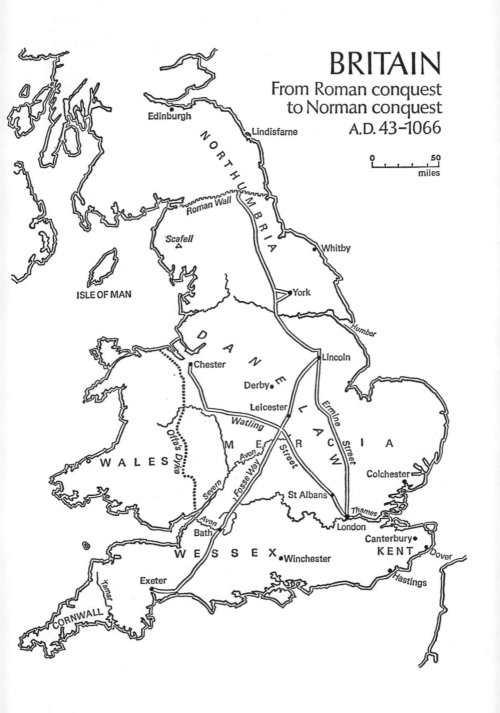

BRITAIN
From Roman conquest
to Norman conquest
A.D. 43–1066

0   50
miles

Edinburgh
Lindisfarne
NORTHUMBRIA
Roman Wall
Scafell △
Whitby
ISLE OF MAN
York
Humber
D A N E
Chester
Lincoln
Derby
Leicester
Ermine Street
L A W
Watling
Olfa's Dyke
M E R C I A
Avon
Street
WALES
Fosse Way
Severn
Colchester
St Albans
Thames
Avon
London
Bath
Canterbury
WESSEX
Winchester
KENT
Dover
Exeter
Hastings
Tamar
CORNWALL

PREFACE

THIS SHORT BOOK is written for the general reader, for the amateur in the best and original sense of the word, a lover of a subject. It is also an attempt to awaken interest in those who have never given much, or any, thought to the wonder that language is, and the strange adventures of the English tongue.

In it I have tried to show briefly, and without the complexities of linguistics, how the sounds that make speech are formed, and how they were ultimately made visible as written symbols, the letters of the alphabet; how the Teutonic tongue of the conquering Anglo-Saxons supplanted the Celtic speech of the Britons in England, and how, after being simplified by the Viking and Norman invasions, it was almost transfigured by the adoption of countless French and Latin words. I hope this brief history will encourage readers to explore further and, when they turn to a dictionary, look up not only the meaning of a word, but also its derivation, from everyday monosyllables like *pen, ink, write, book* to polysyllabic abstractions like *etymology* and *influenza*.

It seems to me that illustrations can be particularly helpful, for a language is the product and reflection of history as a whole, and its history cannot be treated in isolation. Thus, an inscription from Aquae Sulis or Verulamium, Bath or St Albans, summarizes the Roman occupation of Britain, and the Lindisfarne Gospels the return of Latin after two barbaric centuries. In the same way a Norman castle and cathedral symbolize the subjection of the English tongue to French, Perpendicular Gothic its re-emergence as a literary medium and the language of Chaucer, the Queen's House at Greenwich and Pilgrim Fathers in America the influx of new words from Renaissance Europe and a New World, the dome of St Paul's the advent of the Augustan Age.

Perhaps a word should be added about Richard Carew (1555–1620). A Cornishman of aristocratic Norman descent, he was a friend of Sir Philip Sidney, author of a minor classic, *The Survey of Cornwall* (1602), and of the first literary reference to Shakespeare—in his essay on "The Excellencie of the English Tongue".

THE EXCELLENCY OF THE
ENGLISH TONGUE

INTRODUCTION

IN APRIL 1605 Richard Carew wrote to Sir Robert Cotton to say that he had just come across William Camden's *Remaines of a greater worke concerning Britaine*, a book that he had read with delight, one of the things that pleased him most being the derivations of names, and he expressed the hope that Camden would "prosecute this beginning to a thorough accomplishment in all our other words". Carew, who lived at Antony in southeast Cornwall, had a passion for languages—he had taught himself five—and in his recently published *Survey of Cornwall* had attempted to give the English equivalent of a number of Cornish place-names. He felt so strongly about the virtues of the English language, as written by the friend of his Oxford days, Sir Philip Sidney, and by the new man Shakespeare, that he wrote to Camden himself:

The first and principal point sought in every language is that we may express the meaning of our minds aptly each to other. Next, that we may do it readily, without great ado. Then fully, so as others may thoroughly conceive us. And last of all handsomely, that those to whom we speak may take pleasure in hearing us; so as whatsoever tongue will gain the race of perfection must run on these four wheels: *Significancy, Easiness, Copiousness,* and *Sweetness*; of which the two foremost import a necessity, the two latter a delight.

Now, if I can prove that our English language, for all or the most, is matchable, if not preferable before any other in use at this day, I hope the assent of any impartial reader will pass on my side.

Carew's brief development of his theme so pleased Camden that he published the letter in the second edition of his *Remaines* as *The Excellencie of the English Tongue*, a phrase taken from William Harrison's *Description of Britaine* (1587), which Carew as well as Camden had read.

It is not the purpose of this book to try to prove that the English tongue excels all other living languages in significancy, easiness, copiousness and sweetness. Only a scholar and poet with a profound and prolonged knowledge of a score of languages and their literatures could form a valid opinion, and such a man does not, and never will, exist. But it is possible to show that, despite certain defects and deficiencies, the English tongue does possess these virtues in more than common measure.

But what is the English tongue? the English language? To answer indirectly, here is the first verse of a German poem by Goethe, "Erlkönig":

> Wer reitet so spät durch Nacht und Wind?
> Es ist der Vater mit seinem Kind;
> Er hat den Knaben wohl in dem Arm,
> Er fasst ihn sicher, er hält ihn warm.

Five of the words are English as well as German—*so, wind, in, arm, warm*—and an Englishman knowing no German might guess at a few more: *und, ist, hat* are probably *and, is, has*; *Nacht* may be *night*, though *Vater* (father) may be mistaken for *water*. And the three forms of the masculine definitive article (instead of the constant English *the*) will be puzzling: nominative *der*, accusative *den*, dative *dem*.

And now the first verse of a French poem by Victor Hugo:

> Lorsque l'enfant paraît, le cercle de famille
> Applaudit à grands cris. Son doux regard qui brille
> Fait briller tous les yeux,
> Et les plus tristes fronts, les plus souillés peut-être,
> Se dérident soudain à voir l'enfant paraître,
> Innocent et joyeux.

Although there are only four words spelled as in English— *regard, plus, fronts, innocent*—an Englishman ignorant of French would at once pick out (though mistake the meaning of *fronts* and *dérident*—foreheads and unfurrow): *infant, circle, family, applaud, deride, joyous* and perhaps *sudden*. It is worth noting that all but two of these words have two or three syllables, whereas the German words are all monosyllabic.

Then, part of "A Charm for Catching a Swarm of Bees", in the English of more than a thousand years ago:

> Sitte ge, sigewif, sigað to eorþan!
> næfre ge wilde to wudu fleogan!
> Beo ge swa gemindige mines godes
> swa bið manna gehwilc metes and eðeles.

Here are three recognizable modern English words: *sit, to, wild*. But *wild* is also a German word, and a German reader would recognize *fleogan* as *fliegen* (fly), *mines* as *meines* (of my), *manna* as *Mann* (man), and *sige* and *gemindige* would have a familiar ring. To him the passage might mean more than to the Englishman, but to the Frenchman it would mean nothing at all.

Finally, the first verse of a poem by W. H. Auden:

> Look, stranger, at this island now
> The leaping light for your delight discovers,
> Stand stable here
> And silent be,
> That through the channels of the ear
> May wander like a river
> The swaying sound of the sea.

The German would know *stand, wander,* and probably recognize *light, here, and, sea*; but the Frenchman would know *stable, silent,* and ought to recognize *stranger, discovers, river,* and perhaps *channels*: again, all words of more than one syllable.

This, then, is the English tongue: originally and fundamentally a Teutonic language, to which has been added within the last 1,000 years a vocabulary of longer French words. This also is a summary of its history, which is even more briefly summarized in the words *tongue* and *language*, the first the Old English *tunge* (German *Zunge*), the other the *langage* of Old French, and *lingua* of Latin.

And yet, the words can only symbolize, not summarize, the story of the English tongue; and the history of the language that was once merely the speech of a handful of invading barbarians, and is now not only the speech but also the written and printed word of millions of civilized, more or less civilized,

people all over the globe, deserves a more detailed considera-
tion. For the strange adventures and vicissitudes of the English
tongue are a reflection of the political, social and cultural
history of Britain, and beyond that, of countries and continents
to which it has been taken in the last 400 years: from America
to India, from Africa to Australia. And after all, English is the
language of Chaucer and Shakespeare, of Keats and Hardy,
and a full appreciation of any literature depends to some degree
on an appreciation, an understanding, of the language in which
it is written.

But more than that: an appreciation, an understanding, of
language. One of the chief aims, perhaps the chief aim, of
education is, or should be, to rouse the faculty of wonder, to
launch the mind on strange seas of imagination, on voyages of
discovery and exploration of the visible and invisible wonders
of the world. Most of us take language for granted, but suppose
we had grown up on some remote island, without parents or
elders to teach us to speak, without any knowledge of the outside world, what sort of creatures should we be? We should not
know how to light a fire, for we should not know what fire is;
much less should we know how to cook, for we should have no
pots, and probably little food. Sun and moon, day and night,
tides and running water would all be inexplicable mysteries,
and mysteries they would remain for our children. We should
be, or rather, our lives would be more primitive than those of
the most primitive men of the Old Stone Age; for they knew
how to make stone implements, and were skilled in the art of
hunting, and because they could speak, they could transmit
their little knowledge to their children. But we should have no
speech, no articulate sounds with which to communicate, and
most of our little acquired knowledge, and all our thought,
would perish with us.

If one aim of education is to rouse the faculty of wonder,
wonder in the infinite immensity of the universe with its
galaxies receding beyond light's horizon, in the infinitesimal
particles that go to make up matter, in the emergence of life,
and of man from the slime, our wonder should also be roused
by the achievement that has made possible his accumulation of
knowledge, and his spiritual and modest moral evolution—
speech.

I

SPEECH

CAREW DEFINED SPEECH as "the expression of the mind's perception by the voice", and was right to think of language as speech rather than as writing. No doubt he was unaware of this, for he wrote two and a half centuries before the publication of the *Origin of Species* and its revelation of the antiquity and evolution of man. For Carew, as for Shakespeare, man had been created a few thousand years before his time, a perfect creature in the image of God, endowed with the gift of speech, and presumably with that of writing as well. Then, after the days of Noah, when people began to multiply, came the Babel affair, when the Lord confounded their single speech, shredding it into Hebrew, Greek, Latin, French, English and the rest, so that they could no longer understand one another. It makes a good story, but the truth, or what must be approximately the truth, is far more wonderful.

Some two million years ago, perhaps, the glimmerings of conscious mind, an awareness of self and environment, began to flicker in the brain of the ape-like creature that was to evolve into man. He could probably communicate with his companions by signs, gestures and elementary noises, by pointing, nodding, grimacing, perhaps even smiling, by grunts, exclamations and shouts; but dawning consciousness would lead to the invention of sounds more significant, which in their turn would stimulate his mental development.

Without speech there could have been little or no progression of thought, for thought must have something in which to clothe itself, symbols that fix the elusive concept, and with which the mind can build. Moreover, the ability to communicate meant interchange of information and ideas, the pooling of knowledge and thought, and their transmission to the next generation. Speech stimulated thought, and knowledge became, within a limited circle, cumulative. It is the most wonderful of man's accomplishments, for it is fundamental, the source and spring of his triumphant progress.

We can only guess how language developed during the hundreds of thousands of years that it must have taken to evolve into articulate speech, from what, to begin with, can have been little more than a baby's babble. Perhaps the naming of concrete things came first: parts of the body, people, animals, plants, sun and the rest of the visible world. Next, perhaps, sounds that symbolized action: eating, running, throwing, and so on, and sounds descriptive of things and actions—big, little, fast, slow—and eventually subsidiary sounds that linked names, actions and characterization into simple units of expression. We should not think of these sounds as words and sentences, but as a succession of more or less intelligible noises, too fluid and amorphous for grammatical analysis. Even today, although we write words separately, we do not normally speak them separately, butrunthemtogether pausingonlyattheendofaphrase orclause. But when speech had reached this stage of communication about the physical environment, it would be possible to develop means of expressing ideas about the invisible, intangible world, about such abstractions as birth, life, sickness and death.

Whatever happened, however language evolved, there can be little doubt that our ancestors of 20,000 years ago, the big-brained hunters of the last Ice Age, were able to speak fluently to one another. From the rigours of the arctic climate they took shelter in caves, on the walls of which, by the dim light of rush candles, they painted pictures of the animals they hunted: deer, bison, bulls and woolly rhinoceros, which for vigour and sureness of line have never been surpassed. These artists must have had a language, possibly one of some complexity, for the grammar of a primitive tongue is often surprisingly elaborate. Their vocabulary would inevitably be small, restricted to their own limited environment and experience, though some of their words may have expressed ideas and emotions: fear, anger, hatred, affection, love. No doubt they sang as they danced about their fires, songs that were the audible equivalent of the magic paintings on their walls, and composed and recited myths to account for the mysteries about them.

Save in knowledge and experience, these artists of the Old Stone Age were not so very different from us and, thanks to the power of speech, they were very different from the other animals. Not only could they communicate freely with one another, even in the darkness of their caves, not only could they describe their adventures, explain their thoughts and feelings, and derive pleasure from the stringing together of sounds in speech and song, but knowledge, transmitted from generation to generation, was accumulating: flint implements were improved, and eventually gave place to bronze; hunting was superseded by farming, a momentous revolution involving the change from a nomadic to a settled way of life; the arts of pottery and weaving were devised; and perhaps some 6,000 years ago, men began to make visible symbols for the sounds of their speech.

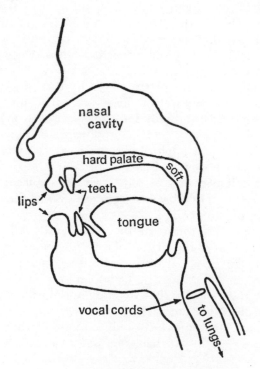

THE ORGANS OF SPEECH

Wonderful as is man's invention of language, the mechanism of speech, the way in which it is produced, is easily understood. When we breathe normally, air is drawn in through the nostrils, along the passage above the palate, and down the windpipe to the lungs, whence it is expelled by the same route. At times of unusual physical exertion, as when climbing a steep hill or running, the lungs need more air, and we gulp it in and blow it out through the much greater cavity of the mouth. If exertion is so great that it causes distress and exhaustion, our panting is accompanied by a noise that is something more than the mere expulsion of air: *u–u–u*. This is voice, produced in the larynx, or Adam's apple (where a piece of the forbidden fruit stuck in our ancestor's throat) at the top of the windpipe.

Across the larynx, from front to back, are stretched the vocal cords, two muscular ligaments, their outer edges attached to the sides but their inner edges free, rather like the skin of a drum slit up the middle. These two membranes can be drawn wide apart, as when we breathe freely, or drawn together to stop the breath, or partially opened, so that they vibrate and make a noise when air from the lungs is forced through the gap between them. This can be simulated by the lips. If open, the breath can pass freely out of the mouth; if firmly closed, the breath is stopped; but if only loosely closed, a strong expulsion of breath will force the lips to vibrate rapidly. The shorter the cords the higher the pitch of the voice, as the vibrations are faster, those of a woman being some 300 a second, a man's only about half as many. At puberty a girl's voice deepens and a boy's voice "breaks", because of the growth of the larynx and lengthening of the cords.

The unamplified sound of the vocal cords would be thin and reedy as that of the strings of a violin without the wooden instrument that gives it resonance. But man is a musical instrument, and it is the chest and hollows of the head, the mouth and nasal cavity, that magnify and enrich vocal sound.

Many of the other animals have voice, from mouse's squeak to lion's roar, but man is the only creature to have acquired the power of speech, which is essentially the ability to modify voice into a variety of sounds that can be combined into intelligible patterns. The agent that modifies voice is the tongue, and the importance of the tongue as the organ of speech is acknow-

cf ᚱᚢᚾᚴ

ledged, unconsciously perhaps, by our use of the word as a
synonym for language, itself derived from Latin *lingua*, meaning
both *tongue* and *language*.

The mouth is vaulted by the palate, which is hard from the
ridge just above the upper teeth until, towards the back, it
softens and terminates in the pendent uvula. The hard palate
is fixed, but the soft palate is movable. When lowered, it closes
the mouth cavity, so that air from the lungs can escape only
along the nasal passage above the palate and through the
nostrils. When raised, the air can be expelled through mouth
and lips.

If words are set to music, it is the vowels, not the consonants,
that form the notes, which may be almost indefinitely prolonged; and vowels, particularly long vowels, form the basic
music of speech. The word is derived from Latin *vox*, meaning
voice, and all vowels are "voiced", produced by the voice. But
each vowel sound is determined by the position of the tongue
in relation to the palate, or rather, of the thick, fleshy middle
and back of the tongue, for the tip has nothing to do with vowel
formation. Thus, if the tongue is drawn back as far as possible,
and raised almost to touch the soft palate, we get the *oo* of *moon*.
If the middle is pushed forward as far as possible, so that it
almost touches the hard palate, we get the *ee* of *lee*. If the mouth
is now opened wide from the smiling position of *ee*, with tongue
still forward, but low, we have the *a* of *man*, and if drawn back
to the low position we have the long *ah* that reveals the back
of the throat. If now we say slowly and deliberately *coo-ee-a-ha*
we can feel, as it were, the four corners of the quadrilateral of
the mouth where these vowels are formed, and trace the boundaries of voice.

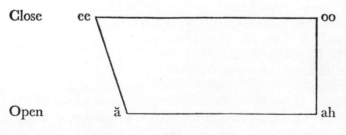

Close   ee   oo

Open   ă   ah

As these are extreme positions of the tongue, back-forward, up-down, all other vowel sounds must lie either on or within the quadrilateral. Thus, at the front, at equal distances between *ee* and short *ă* lie the half-close long *ā* of *lay* and half-open short *ĕ* of *men*. Then at the back, between the cooing *oo* and gaping *ah* lie the long half-close *ō* of *low* and half-open *aw* of *law*. Again, we can feel the formation of these vowels if we open the mouth in the stages: *ee-ā-ĕ-ă, oo-ō-aw-ah.*

Front	Hard palate	Soft palate	Back

Close ee	i	u	oo
Half-close ā		er	ō
Half-open ĕ		ŭ	aw
Open ă			ah

These are the eight cardinal, or principal, vowels, formed by the tongue when working hard and quickly at the limits of back and front. But the English are not given to extremes, and our tongues do not exert themselves unduly, so that our long vowels merely approach the cardinal positions. The French are more eager and energetic in their speech, and the long *e, ā, ō, oo* of their *lit, lait, l'eau, loup* are the extremes to which the lazy, lingering vowels of *lee, lay, low, loo* only approximate. Similarly, the short *a* of standard English *man* is only a little below the *e* of *men*, because we do not go to the full downward position of German *Mann* and Yorkshireman's pronunciation of the word.

Most of the English vowels, therefore, lie within the diagram. The neutral short *ŭ* of the unmodified voice lies near the bottom centre, where the tongue is at rest. It resembles, but is fainter than the *u* of *up*, as can be observed in the pronunciation of *upper*. It is a very common sound in English, that of the indefinite and definite article before a consonant—*a man, the man*—and heard in such words as *above, upon*, and final *er* of *father*. If we raise the tongue a little, we have the real *er* sound of hesitation in speech, and of *pert, girl, curt, word*, while higher up towards the back is the *u* of *pull*, and somewhere towards the close front is the short *i* of *it*.

We must say "somewhere", for only sounds made with the tongue fully forward and fully back can be accurately charted, and no two people pronounce in exactly the same way all the sounds that lie within the diagram, or even on its boundaries. My pronunciation of such a word as "idealization" will differ slightly from the reader's, and the broad Yorkshire and Cockney versions differ wildly.

The northerner is often contemptuous of the southerner's pronunciation, in which *man* sounds to him like *men*, and *lad* like *led*, though the northerner's *where* may sound like *weir* or *we're* to the southerner. Such ambiguity is obviously important, and the smallest unit of speech that can cause a semantic change, a change of meaning, is called a phoneme. Thus, in "refained" English, a *pint* of beer is a *paint*, while the Cockney does not *paint* his cart, but *pints* it. Phonemic boundaries are vague, and it can be appreciated how easily the pronunciation of a language, particularly of its long vowels, may change over the years: why the *tay* that Pope celebrated in Queen Anne's reign could change to *tea*.

Tay, like *paint*, has in fact two vowels, short *e* gliding towards short *i* within the diagram, and because the English do not push their tongues to extremes, and tend to linger over long sounds, the language has many of these double vowels, or diphthongs. In saying *how*, for example, the tongue rises from *ah* to *oo*, from bottom to top of the mouth. But the commonest diphthongs are those in which the tongue sinks to the neutral *u*, as in *peer*, *pair*, *pour*, *poor*, where it is represented by *r*. *Our*, therefore, is a triphthong, a treble vowel, *ah-oo-ŭ*.

As a result, English is very rich in vowel sounds lying within the limits of *coo-ee–a-ha*:

at	men	bit	on	up
art	see	*bite*	*lone*	(upp)er
all	pert	*fire*	*roar*	put
air	*peer*		*boil*	June
bay			house	*sure*
			hour	

27

Here are 23 vowel sounds, of which seven are short and sixteen long; and of these sixteen, nine are diphthongs and two (*fire, hour*) triphthongs. Obviously the five vowel symbols of the alphabet cannot represent all the vowel sounds of the English language. How could a foreigner beginning to learn English possibly know how to pronounce the vowels even in this easy sentence, with its *how, know; could, -nounce; Eng-, -els, even, -reign; learn, easy*? A much more elaborate code of symbols is needed by those whose business it is to chart the sounds of speech, a phonetic alphabet with an unambiguous symbol for each one.

In theory, it would be possible to compose a language entirely of vowels, but in practice such a speech would be laboured, monotonous and barely intelligible, as each significant sound would lie so close to its neighbours that it would often be confused with them. Vowels form the body of a language, giving it breadth and tone, but to avoid confusion there must not be too many; they must be unambiguous, and separated, as well as reinforced, by sounds made in other ways. This is the work of the consonants, which change the meaning of a vowel sound: *b*, for example, distinguishing *bay* from *day, gay, hay* and the rest. A vowel can make a syllable, but a consonant cannot (save in such words as *chasm, rhythm*); it must be sounded with a vowel, as its Latin derivation implies: *consonare*, to sound together.

Vowel sounds are the modification of voice in its free passage through the mouth, by the thick, fleshy middle and back of the tongue, and to make sounds that can be distinguished from them, other means have to be devised, and other agents used. These are, principally, the lips, teeth and thin, nimble blade and tip of the tongue, which restrict or temporarily obstruct the breath, the friction of its escape through a narrow passage causing a hiss, its sudden release a mild explosion. Most consonants, therefore, are formed at the front of the mouth, and add a sibilant or percussive element to the vowel music. As sounds that can be formed in this way are limited, their number is increased by having a voiced as well as an unvoiced version of some of them. Thus, if we say *s-s-s-s*, we hear only the hiss of the escaping breath, but change to *z-z-z-z*, and we hear also the vibration of the vocal cords—voice.

Because some consonants are so nearly related, and others mere breath at the front of the mouth, they are less resonant, more fleeting and elusive than vowels, more difficult to hear. There is an old story of a message passed down a line of soldiers by their commander: "I am going to advance; send me reinforcements." This emerged at the end of the line as: "I am going to a dance; lend me three and fourpence." The vowels were intact, but some of the consonants had gone astray; and unless consonants are distinctly pronounced, the partially deaf have to invent substitutes that fit the vowels that they hear, so that "Alfred Wallis" may become "alcoholic". We may, then, imagine the vowels as full, voiced sounds reverberating under the vaulted palate at the centre and back of the mouth, while the thin consonants hiss and cluck and chatter at the front, where the blade of the tongue is active.

There are three pairs of consonants that are plosives formed by the stoppage and sudden release of the breath, the first one of each pair being unvoiced, the second voiced. For *p* and *b*, the breath is stopped by the lips; for *t* and *d* by the blade of the tongue pressing against the teeth-ridge; for *k* and *g*, by the back of the tongue pressing against the soft palate. The last pair are gutturals, formed in the throat and, with the allied *-ng* of words like *sing*, exceptions to the front-of-the-mouth formation of English consonants.

The trio *m*, *n*, *-ng* are formed in the same way as *b*, *d*, *g*, but the dropped soft palate diverts the breath from the mouth, so that most of it passes through the nasal cavity and out at the nose. A bad cold that blocks the nose prevents the proper pronunciation of these nasal consonants, which revert to their *b*, *d*, *g* form, so that "Mary never sings" becomes something like "Bary dever sigs".

The hisses of the breath's restricted passage form pairs of unvoiced and voiced fricatives. Thus, *f* and *v* are the air escaping when the upper teeth touch the lower lip; the *th* of *thin* and *dh* of *then*, when the tongue is placed between the teeth. For *s* and *z*, the air escapes round the tongue when its tip just touches the teeth-ridge; for the *sh* of *shall* and *zh* of *measure*, between the hard palate and raised middle of the tongue.

Allied to *sh* and *zh* are *tsh* (*ch*) and *dzh* (*j*), the stopped breath after *t* and *d* being released more slowly, as in *church*, *catch*, and in *jar*. There are no single letters in the alphabet to represent *sh, zh, tsh* (or *ng, th, dh*), and even *dzh* is not always represented by *j*, but often by *g, ge* and *dge*, as in *giant, George, judge*.

There are five consonants—*h, l, r, w, y*—that are formed with little or no stoppage or friction of the breath, and have a way of sometimes being seen and not heard, sometimes heard but not seen.

The aspirate *h*, as its name implies (Latin *aspirare*, to breathe), is the unvoiced, unstopped expulsion of air from the lungs. As a single consonant, it occurs only at the beginning of a syllable and before a vowel (*behave*), and is generally pronounced, though not in *heir, hour, honour*, and not always in *hotel*: words taken from the French, in which *h* is always silent. It is worth noting the relation between *h* and *sh*, as in *hush*, where the unrestricted breath is finally checked by the raised tongue.

The liquid *l* is the half-stopped breath escaping when the tongue is removed from the tooth-ridge. In some words it is no longer sounded, but Chaucer gave *l* its full value in such words as *ha-l-f, pa-l-mer, fo-l-k*. In the same way, *r* has often disappeared in speech, as in *disappear, form*, and the termination *-er*. When pronounced, it is formed in much the same way as *l*, though the tongue is slightly curled and does not quite touch the teeth-ridge, as can be felt by saying *lorry*. The oriental finds it difficult to distinguish between the *r* and *l* of standard English, and might well say *lolly*, though he could scarcely mistake the robust, rolled *r* of the Scot for an *l*.

Both *r* and *l* are voiced, and so is *w*, for it is a semi-vowel, the echo, as it were, made by the pouting lips after saying *oo*: *oo(w)et* (wet). It is a ghostly whispering sound, particularly in its unvoiced form of *wh*: *what, white*; and it even vanishes in *who*, yet returns unseen in *one*.

Finally, *y* is a substitute for *i* in *sky* and *lady*, and a semi-vowel in *yes, young*, where it is the echo of long *e*: *ee-es, ee-oung*. Here it is voiced, but in its unvoiced state it is heard without being seen in, for example, *hew* and *huge*.

Consonants may be classified in another way:

LABIALS, formed by the lips: *p, b, m, w, f, v*.
LIQUIDS, by the tongue on the teeth-ridge: *l, r, n*.

DENTALS, by the tongue and teeth: *t, d*; *th, dh.*

SIBILANTS, by the tongue's restriction of the breath: *s, z*; *sh, zh*; *ch, j.*

GUTTURALS, by the back of the tongue in the throat: *k, g, -ng.*

These similarities of formation are important, for much of the beauty of prose and verse is dependent on the interplay of related consonants.

These, then, are the principal vowel and consonantal sounds of the English tongue, some 50, twice as many as the letters of the alphabet: sounds that either singly or in combination make words, which in their turn make speech. They also make poetry; for the combining of words and their sounds, not only what they mean but also what they suggest, is the art of the poet, as the harmonious combination of notes is that of the musician. The word *bronze,* for example, means an alloy of copper and tin, and gives us a mental image of a brown metal, but with it there will probably be other associations: a coin or a medal, the Ghiberti baptistery doors or a Rodin sculpture, bronze-age weapons and ornaments, any one of which may lead to remoter associations: Mycenae, Stonehenge, Florence, Dante, Browning, our schooldays, patina, domes, Sevastopol. But more than this, there is a peculiar fitness in the sound of *bronze* as the spoken symbol of the metal: the short *o* suggests its strength, that it is *strong,* as the initial *br* and prolonged buzz of the final *nz* suggest its gong-like resonance.

There can be few words that have as many associations as *sleep,* yet no poet is likely to write a lyric based on words that begin with *sl.* For some reason or other, most English words, many of them Scandinavian in origin, with these initial letters have unpleasant meanings and associations, as a glance at the dictionary will show: *slabber, slag, slander, slattern, slaughter, slaver, sleazy, sleight, slick, slime, slink, slit, slither, slobber, slop, sloth, slouch, sloven, sludge, slug . . .,* and nobody would suggest *slump* or *slush* as a substitute for *bronze.*

Many words are onomatopoeic, or imitative: *cuckoo, crash, mutter,* and certain sounds are more subtly symbolic: *sl-* seeming to suggest poverty, dirt, dankness, trickery and crawl-

31

ing ooze. More happily, the season of spring is symbolized by
the rapid short consonants and single short vowel of the word,
autumn by its long mellow vowel followed by the neutral *u*.
Shakespeare, celebrating youth and beauty in his early, lyrical
poetry, delighted in consonants, particularly in the interplay
of labials, *p*, *b*, *m*, *w*, *f*, *v*, and the liquid *l*:

> Nor did I wonder at the lily's white,
> Nor praise the deep vermilion in the rose;
> They were but sweet, but figures of delight,
> Drawn after you, you pattern of all those.

Later, however, he drew on the unrivalled store of English
vowels for the dramatic poetry of his tragedies:

> Where souls do couch on flowers, we'll hand in hand,
> And with our sprightly port make the ghosts gaze:
> Dido and her Aeneas shall want troops,
> And all the haunt be ours.

Some measure of the variety of sounds in the English language.

WRITING

SPEECH IS THE most wonderful of all man's accomplishments, for it is fundamental, the beginning of his spiritual pilgrimage. Without speech, only the most elementary forms of communication would have been possible, and without words in which to express his observations, experiences and thoughts, his mental evolution and inventive progress would have been slow indeed. But speech is ephemeral, words are mere breath, no sooner heard than gone, and before the invention of writing their only repository was in the memories of the few who heard them. Today it is different, for speech has conquered space and time; microphone and radio make audiences of millions, and an astronaut can address the world from the mountains of the moon. Then, owing to the invention of phonograph, gramophone and tape recorder, our descendants of a thousand years hence will be able to hear how we speak in the twentieth century. But the word phonograph (sound-writer) is misleading, for these instruments do not write, but merely record and reproduce speech and other sounds. It is true that on film and television we can hear the words and see the speaker, but this is only the echo and shadow of these things. Recorded speech is not writing: a permanent, visual representation of the sounds of speech.

Without writing, these discoveries and inventions—radio, television and the rest—could never have been made, for such ingenuities depend on the deep accumulation of knowledge and ideas permanently recorded in manuscript and printed page, so that each successive generation can stand, as it were, on the shoulders of its predecessor, and begin where it left off.

As we take speech, so we take writing for granted, and it is worth pausing to consider the wonder that writing really is. A spoken word is merely a sound, a symbol that normally bears no resemblance to the thing to which it refers. The sound sun in no way resembles the bright disc in the sky, nor is there any relation between the sound time and the concept that it stands for. But neither do the written words sun and time in any way resemble the sounds, the spoken words, that they stand for. The written word is at two removes from the object: in speech the visible sun is transformed into a sound, and then in writing again made visible in an abstract form. And an abstraction—time—is first made audible, then visible as another abstraction. The written word is a symbol of a symbol, the shadow of a shade.

It is true that some of our words are onomatopoeic in origin, imitative, suggestive of the things or qualities they represent. Obviously buzz and cuckoo are imitations of sounds, and it has already been suggested that initial *sl-* seems to imply sluggishness and slime, *spr-* the tautness of spring, sprout, spruce, spry, and that bronze gives the impression of strength and resonance. In the same way shiver, shudder, tremble, are all suggestive of quivering, and long vowels are warmer than short ones. Cold is an exception, as warm as gold, but in Old English it was *cald*, resembling the German *kalt*. Moreover, most of the letters of our alphabet are derived from pictorial representations: A comes from the drawing of an ox's head, whence the Greek name *alpha*, from the Semitic *aleph*, ox; B, *beta*, from Semitic *beth*, a house; and so on. But these origins, onomatopoeic or pictorial, have long been forgotten: the letters of our alphabet are abstract symbols, and today few of the words they represent are obviously imitative of appearance, sound or quality.

No wonder the transformation of speech into graphic form was a late invention in man's history, and associated with magic. Not only was the concept of changing sound into visible symbols an immense imaginative leap, but there was also the physical difficulty. Without something to write on and something to write with, progress was bound to be slow. The first real writing material was papyrus, made from a reed by the Egyptians some 5,000 years ago. They also prepared parchment from the skins of animals, and this was the principal material used outside Egypt until about AD 750, when the Arabs spread abroad a knowledge of paper, invented by the Chinese at the beginning of the Christian era. Some 20,000 years before the invention of papyrus, late palaeolithic man represented the things he talked about by painting them on the walls of caves; pictures of his essential occupation, hunting—almost certainly a form of sympathetic magic, for the depiction of a hunted animal transfixed with arrows meant the killing of a real one on the morrow. Other less gifted peoples than the Ice-Age artists had to content themselves with scratching or daubing the surface of rocks, stones and bones, making rudimentary representations of visible objects.

These pictograms were the first and most obvious form of writing, and may, indeed, as scratches in the soil, have helped man to evolve a spoken language. But they were not writing in the true sense; they were not symbols of the sounds that themselves symbolized the objects. The interposition of speech was omitted, and the drawing was a direct representation of the visible thing. A circle might represent the sun, a wavy line water, a few straight lines a man. Medieval stained glass is pictographic: the story of St Martin in a series of coloured pictures, for example, was a graphic representation of his life for the benefit of those, the vast majority, who could not read. Even today we find pictograms useful, particularly for giving rapid information on road signs: the silhouette of an aeroplane, children, cattle or a man with a shovel indicating what may lie ahead. The great advantage of the pictogram is its independence of language, so that it may be understood by people of any nationality. Its great disadvantage is its limited range. It would, for example, be very difficult to represent pictographically the meaning of this simple sentence.

The pictogram was essentially realistic, the representation of a visible object, and its natural development was towards abstraction: the representation of intangible and invisible things in a similar way, of qualities and even thoughts. The pictogram thus became the ideogram, in which an eye or an ear might symbolize looking or listening, and a circle might mean the quality of brightness or heat, as well as the visible sun. Such multiple meanings obviously led to ambiguity, and some sort of addition had to be made to the sun circle to indicate brightness. The Chinese, whose writing is still basically ideographic, add the moon symbol, which was originally a semi-circle. *Big* is the symbol of a man with arms outstretched,

35

大 and such abstractions as *above, below, middle* are 上, 下, 中.
More delightfully, and cynically, the triple symbol of a woman
signifies noise or quarrel.

Chinese is a monosyllabic language, the written characters
of which are more or less conventionalized pictorial representations of things or ideas. This gives great scope for cal-
ligraphy, but it means that there are inevitably thousands of
symbols, and, as the number of monosyllables is limited, the
sound may have a number of quite different meanings. To
distinguish them, therefore, two characters are combined, one
indicating the concept, the other its pronunciation, as we might
represent sea by wavy lines for water, followed by an eye,
indicating see. The water could not then be mistaken for a lake
or river, but must be the word pronounced like see.

There is, therefore, a phonetic element in Chinese writing,
but in pure, primitive ideography the symbol does not represent
sound but meaning. The difference can be appreciated by
considering our own use of ideograms. A red triangle sym-
bolizes, but in no way resembles (unless derived from Greek
D, Δ) the sound of the word danger. A T, resembling the
Chinese symbol for not, signifies "no through road", a "cul-
de-sac". The figures 1, 2, 3 do not represent the sound of *one,
two, three,* any more than they represent that of the French
un, deux, trois, or German *ein, zwei, drei.* They are independent
of language, pure ideograms like other arithmetical symbols,
+, ∴, √, =.

The earliest Chinese writing to survive dates from about
1500 BC, but the earliest Egyptian writing is nearly 1,500 years
older. These are the hieroglyphics, or "sacred carved writings",
to be seen on the ruins of their monuments and temples, though
they were also painted on pottery and written on papyrus.
Like Chinese, hieroglyphics were pictograms or ideograms that
were sometimes combined to indicate pronunciation. But in
their writing the Egyptians represented only the consonantal
sounds, the vowels being supplied by the reader from the context,
as we ourselves write ft but read foot or feet according to the
preceding numeral. In this way the Egyptians developed
symbols for groups of consonants, normally three, but sometimes two, and even one.

An even earlier form of writing than Egyptian may have been

that of the Sumerians of Mesopotamia, where stone tablets of about 3200 BC have been found engraved with pictograms. These developed into ideograms, which sometimes represented the syllables of an abstract word pictorially, as we might represent boycott by two simple drawings. Then, as stone was scarce, they impressed their signs on clay with a stylus, a chisel-like instrument, so that all lines were straight, a combination of short lines and triangles. Ideograms thus lost their realism and became merely conventional signs. This was the cuneiform, or wedge-shaped, writing that was adopted by the Assyrians and Babylonians of Mesopotamia.

Both Sumerians and Egyptians, therefore, had gone beyond the mere representation of words, the former by creating symbols that stood for syllables, the latter by symbols that stood for groups of consonants, and even for a single consonant combined with an invisible vowel. Both were close to the ultimate analysis of the spoken word into its smallest components, the sounds that can be represented by letters. Yet neither succeeded in making the final breakthrough.

Appropriately enough, however, the alphabet appears to have been invented halfway between Mesopotamia and Egypt, by a Semitic people of Palestine or Syria, where clay tablets have been found inscribed in an alphabet of 32 letters. The writing is cuneiform, but the inspiration was probably Egyptian, for the Semites, like the Egyptians, considered consonants the essential structure of words, and could the more easily appreciate the convention of a symbol for a consonant plus an unidentified vowel, and apply it to their own language. These alphabetic inscriptions date from about 1400 BC, though there may be earlier ones, so that by the time Stonehenge was being completed in Britain, somebody in the Near East had invented a system of writing in which the symbols no longer represented things or ideas, or even words or syllables, but each separate sound that goes to make up speech—letters.

The invention of the alphabet was a momentous one, for letters are the simplest and most efficient form of visual communication. An ideographic script like Chinese needs almost as many symbols as there are words in the language. A syllabary, composed of symbols for every vowel-consonant sound, is much simpler, and the Japanese can manage with 76. But

Japanese words are composed of two-letter syllables, one of their fourteen consonants followed by one of their five vowels, as in such names as Na-ga-sa-ki, Mo-to-no-bu, and English, with its far great-er syll-ab-ic com-plex-it-y, would re-quire a form-id-ab-le num-ber of sym-bols. We manage with only 26 letters, though admittedly these are not enough to represent unambiguously all the sounds in the language.

The early Semitic alphabet was adopted by other Semitic peoples, including the Hebrews and, more important, the Phoenicians. More important, because the Phoenicians were the great merchants of the age, trading throughout the whole length of the Mediterranean, and by the beginning of the ninth century BC their alphabet had been taken over by the Greeks. This application of a Semitic alphabet to a European language was an epoch-making event, for not only was it the beginning of all European alphabetic writing, it was the dawn of European civilization.

Of course the Greeks had to modify the consonantal Phoenician alphabet to suit their own language; they transformed some of the symbols into vowels, and invented others for sounds for which there was no Semitic equivalent, *ph* and *x*, for example, but half of the alphabet they took over with little alteration. And, like the Semites, at first they wrote from right to left, then *boustrophedon*, "as the ox turns in ploughing", alternately from right to left, left to right, and sometimes from bottom to top. By the fifth century BC, however, the great age of Athens, of the drama and visual arts, the Greeks wrote from left to right and top to bottom, and had transformed the Phoenician symbols into the 24 letters of their alphabet.

It was carried farther west by the Etruscans, a mysterious people from Asia Minor who invaded and settled in Italy, north of Rome. Again the alphabet was modified when adapted to their own strange, and still undeciphered language, eventually being reduced to twenty letters: four vowels and sixteen consonants.

By the seventh century BC the Romans had taken over the alphabet of their northern neighbours, and again applied it to a European tongue, to the language that was to become for centuries the common speech of the western world. For a time the Romans wrote from right to left, but then changed direction, and eventually evolved their 23-letter alphabet, the western alphabet of today, though without the letters J, U, W. This was the alphabet of the Latin language that the Romans brought to Britain in the first century AD, and that was to be spoken and written here for nearly four centuries.

3

BRITONS AND ROMANS

FIVE THOUSAND YEARS ago, when writing was being developed in the Near East, Britain was sparsely populated by men of the Middle Stone Age, bands of wandering savages who lived by hunting, fishing and gathering food. Then, about 2500 BC a people who came originally from the eastern Mediterranean crossed from the continent and settled in southern England, men of the New Stone Age bringing with them a revolutionary knowledge of farming, pottery, weaving, and a settled way of life. They were followed a few centuries later by another Mediterranean people, who sailed into the Atlantic, along the coast of Spain and France and up the west coast of Britain, settling and building the great stone tombs that are still to be seen from Malta to Brittany and Denmark, from Cornwall to Ireland and the Orkneys. Other immigrants followed, notably the Beaker Folk (so called from the characteristic shape of their drinking-vessels) who landed on the east coast. Intermarriage would stimulate their skills, and before they had finished the building of Stonehenge, half temple, half observatory, c. 1500 BC, the Bronze Age had begun.

The peace of the uneventful thousand years of the Bronze Age in Britain was broken when another people began to arrive: the Celts from the region of the Netherlands. To begin with they were not numerous, and farmers like the natives rather than conquerors, but immigration became invasion when, at the beginning of the third century BC, bands of Celtic warriors from central Europe occupied France and landed in Britain. The short, dark, bronze-weaponed inhabitants were no match for these tall, fair, muscular warriors with their iron swords, and either perished or fled into the mountains of the north and west. It may be that the earlier Celtic settlers fled with them, for there were two main types of Celt in Britain: the Goidels or Gaels of Scotland and Ireland, and the Brythons who occupied the southern part of the country, and gave their name to the islands. By the end of the third century BC, therefore, Britain was a Celtic country, though some of the natives survived, and their descendants are still to be found, mainly in Ireland, Scotland, Wales and Cornwall.

What language they spoke we do not know but, as some came originally from the eastern Mediterranean, it may have belonged to the Hamitic family, like Egyptian, or to the Semitic, like Arabic and Hebrew. If so, it was very different from the speech that superseded it, for Celtic, like most other European tongues, was descended from an old European language. There were, however, two main dialects of Celtic speech in Britain. The Brythonic Celts minded their *p*'s, the Goidelic their *q*'s, or rather their *k*'s, so that for the one the old European *quennos*, head, became *cenn*, for the other *pen*, the first syllable of so many place-names in Wales and Cornwall (Penllyn, Penzance), while *Kil-* (cell, chapel) is characteristic of Ireland and Scotland (Killarney, Kilmuir). Again, Latin *quis* and *quattuor*, who and four, are Irish *cia* and *cethir*, but Welsh *pwy* and *petguar*.

When Julius Caesar had subdued the Gauls, the Celts who had occupied France, it was only to be expected that he would next turn his attention to their cousins in Britain. His expeditions of 55 and 54 BC were failures, however, though they opened the way to commercial relations with the country. Then, nearly a hundred years later, in AD 43, the Roman conquest began, and it was not long before England was occupied by the legions. The remoter parts of the islands were too wild and mountainous to be worth the trouble of conquest and settlement; there was no invasion of Ireland; the main routes from Wales were guarded by legionary fortresses, and a great wall was built across the north of England to contain the Celts of Scotland. To the west and north of these outposts of empire the old Celtic way of life went on much as before.

The Roman province of Britannia, therefore, was virtually confined to the more fertile region south of the Wall and east of the Welsh border: to the region that was later to be called England. Here the Romans introduced their civilization; London became their capital, and from it they constructed their straight paved roads along which the legions marched to the fortresses of York, Chester and Caerleon. Crossing them was another great highway running from Lincoln to Exeter, the most westerly fortified camp, or *castra*. Towns such as Verulamium (St Albans) and Aquae Sulis (Bath) were built, and country houses, adorned with frescoes and mosaics. Thus, the southern Britons were brought within the orbit of classical culture, and the long, peaceful centuries as a province of the Empire began.

A similar process was going on in Gaul, but there, nearer the centre of the Empire, it was even more revolutionary; for the Gallic Celts abandoned their own language and adopted the speech of their conquerors from which French is descended. In Britain, however, although the Celtic townspeople, merchants and wealthier class must have spoken much the same kind of Latin as the Gauls, and although several hundred Latin words found their way into the native speech, Latin did not replace Celtic, partly, perhaps, because of intercourse with the unromanized Celts of Wales and Cornwall.

And perhaps it was as a protest against the Roman occupation of part of their islands, symbolized by the Latin alphabet, that the Irish Celts developed their own form of writing, much as, some six centuries later, the Cornish Celts were to erect their crosses as a silent protest against the Saxon invaders of their country. In any event, the Ogham alphabet, so called from its mythical inventor Ogma, originated during the Roman occupation. It had twenty letters—five vowels and fifteen consonants—each represented by from one to five strokes that touched or crossed a medial line.

Although the Celts once occupied the greater part of western Europe, their language has survived only in Ireland, Wales, Scotland, and Brittany, which was colonized later by Celts from Cornwall, where the language died out in the eighteenth century. As a result, Ogham inscriptions are confined to the British Isles, and about 400 have been discovered, most of them in Ireland, some 40 in Wales, and a few in Scotland, the Isle of Man and Cornwall. There is no *p* in the alphabet, but both *c* and *q*, and it looks as though it originated in southern Ireland, where inscriptions are most numerous. But it was a cumbersome form of writing; it served well enough for inscriptions cut in stone, but was no medium for literature, and the Celts adopted the Roman alphabet and writing.

At the beginning of the fourth century, Christianity became the official religion of the Empire, and a British Church was founded. There was not time, however, for widespread conversion to the new faith; the Empire was collapsing, barbarians were attacking its frontiers, the Roman Wall was overrun by the northern Celts, and Saxon pirates were raiding the east coast. In 410 the Romans withdrew, leaving the Britons, civilized and unwarlike after nearly four centuries of Roman peace, at the mercy of the fierce Teutonic pirates.

There followed a dark century of devastation, during which the barbaric invaders advanced across the country, burning towns and villas, and driving the Britons into the Celtic refuges of the west, Wales and Cornwall. The survivors took with them the last vestiges of Roman civilization, Christianity and a knowledge of Latin which, however, was soon forgotten, though a number of borrowed words remained embedded in the language: *medhec* and *kegyn*, for example, representing *medicus* and *coquina*, physician and kitchen.

By 550 Britannia had become England, a devastation in which little or nothing of Rome remained save ruins and the indestructible roads.

4

OLD ENGLISH

THE INVADERS OF Britain who drove the Celts into the west, as the Celts themselves had driven their predecessors, were the Angles, Saxons and Jutes: Teutonic tribes who lived in Frisia and Jutland, the lowlands between the mouth of the Rhine and northern tip of what is now Denmark. They were farmers in search of new territory, fishermen in search of new grounds, sailors for whom piracy was a profitable pastime.

The Jutes were the first to settle: in the south-east, where they established the little kingdom of Kent. The Saxons took over most of the land south of the Thames and Severn estuary, creating the kingdoms of Sussex and Wessex, of the South and West Saxons. Most of the Angles moved north, those in the Midlands forming the kingdom of Mercia, beyond which, north of the Humber, was Northumbria, running up the east side of the country as far as Edinburgh, the town founded later by its king Edwin. Like the Romans, the Anglo-Saxons did not attempt to settle the Celtic north and west, Ireland, the Scottish Highlands and Wales, the land of the *wealas*, or foreigners, as they called the Celts, though in the ninth century Wessex over-ran the other land of foreigners, Corn*wall*.* For the Britons the usurpers were all Saxons, and in Latin the country was at first *Saxonia*; but by the seventh century it was *Anglia*, and as its conquerors called their common language *Englisc*, Latin Anglia became Old English Engla land, the land of the Angles. Chaucer was to write Engelond and Englissh in the late four-teenth century, but soon afterwards (as weng became wing) they assumed their present pronunciation: Ingland, Inglish.

Like Celtic, English is descended from the ancestral Indo-European (or Aryan) language once spoken by a people prob-

* Cf. the surnames: Welsh, *Walsh*; Scottish, *Wallace*; Cornish, *Wallis*. And *walnut* means "foreign nut".

44

ably living in the region east of Poland, who dispersed all over Europe in prehistoric times, some of them even going as far afield as northern India. There they developed the Sanskrit language in which they wrote the Hindu scriptures, the Vedas. These are more than 3,000 years old and, apart from their content, important as the oldest writings in an Indo-European language. Other descendants of the original tongue are Iranian and Balto-Slavic, which includes Russian and Lithuanian, nearest of all, perhaps, to the parent speech.

These, however, had little or no influence on the development of Old English (Anglo-Saxon), which was descended from the Teutonic branch of the family and, with one slight exception, it is only since the occupation of Britain by the English that the language has been modified by two of the other main descendants of the Indo-European tongue. One of these is the Hellenic language of classical Greek literature, the other, and much more important, is Latin, from which in turn are descended the Romance languages of Italian, Spanish, Portuguese and French, the last much the most important direct influence of all.

PRINCIPAL INDO-EUROPEAN LANGUAGES

Indian—Sanskrit

Iranian—Persian

Balto-Slavic—Russian
             Polish
             Lithuanian

Celtic—Goidelic—Gaelic
                Irish

        Brythonic—Welsh
                  Cornish
                  Breton

Hellenic—Greek

Italic—Latin—Italian
             Spanish
             Portuguese
             French

The Excellency of the English Tongue

Teutonic—East—Gothic

   North—Old Norse—Icelandic
                 Swedish
                 Danish
                 Norwegian

   West—Old High German—Modern German
         Old Low German—Dutch

                 Old English—
                 Modern English

The earliest Teutonic writing is Gothic: a fourth-century translation of part of the Bible by Ulfilas, who devised an alphabet for the Goths. High German was the dialect of the centre and south, which after 1500 became the literary language. Low German was spoken in the northern lowlands, the original home of the Anglo-Saxon, or English, invaders of Britain.

As German and English are so nearly related, we should expect them to resemble each other, at least in vocabulary: *Vater*, father; *Name*, name; *bringen*, to bring, *haben*, to have; *grün*, green; *warm*, warm; *drei*, three; *hier*, here; *so*, so; *und*, and. But *father, name, three* (Old English *fæder, nama, thrī*) resemble not only the German, but beyond the Teutonic family they are also Greek *pateer, onoma, treis*, Latin *pater, nomen, tres*, and, even more remotely, Sanskrit *pitr, naman, trayas*. Such resemblances of old words in a number of languages make it clear that all are descended from a common tongue. We have no record of this ancestral language, for its speakers dispersed before the invention of writing, but there can be no doubt that it existed, and was the origin of what is called the Indo-European family of languages.

Languages are always changing, otherwise they are dead. Two centuries ago *fault* rhymed with *fought*, *join* with *line*; the English say *primarily* and *leftenant*, the Americans *primairily* and (more rationally) *lewtenant*. Fourteen centuries ago, *after* the Anglo-Saxon migration to Britain, the Germans of the higher inland country changed initial *d* to *t*, one of the main differences between Low and High German, so that English *day* and *dream*, descended from Low German, are modern High German *Tag* and *Traum*. Much more, then, should we expect changes in a language spoken by different branches of the same people living in ancient times in different places without intercommunication: between eastern and western branches of the Indo-European family, between Indians, Greeks and Romans and barbaric Teutonic tribes. In the word *father*, the main difference between the two groups is the *þ* of the first and *f* of the second; one labial, or lip consonant, has replaced another.

It is easy to understand such interchange of related consonants, for there is little difference in the pronunciation of the labials *p, b, f, v*, or in that of the gutturals *g, k (c)*, or of the dentals *t, d, th*, so that Latin *piscis* is English *fish, frater* is *brother, gelidus* is cold, *tres* is *three*, and Greek *thura* is *door*.

Old English, then, the language spoken by the Anglo-Saxon invaders of Britain, was distantly related to Greek and Latin, but its development in northern Europe had been quite different and, with one slight qualification, was a purely Teutonic speech. Although the Germans were never conquered by the Romans, many of them served in the Roman army, while others lived and worked within the Empire, the frontier of which ran along the Rhine. There was, therefore, considerable intercourse between the two, and even before the Anglo-Saxons invaded Britain they had borrowed a few, some 50, Latin words, mostly connected with war and trade. Among them:

weall, wall, from *vallum*, a rampart.
stræt, from *strata*, as in Watling Street, Ermine Street, the English names for the Roman roads they found in Britain.
mangere, monger, from *mango*, a dishonest trader.
win, wine, from *vinum*, a Mediterranean substitute for the northern *beor* and *meodu*, beer and mead.
flasce, from *flasca*, bottle.
cese, from *caseus*, cheese.
pyle, pillow, from *pulvinus*, cushion.
Sæternesdæg, Saturday, from *Saturni dies*, day of Saturn. The other days of the week are English, but formed after the Latin model: *Thuresdæg*, day of Thor, after *dies Jovis*, day of Jupiter.

When the Anglo-Saxons conquered Britain, they adopted very few Latin words of the Romano-British civilization that they destroyed, and these were mainly connected with place-names. *Port*, from Latin *portus*, probably the Roman name for Portsmouth, may belong to this period, and *wic*, from *vicus*, farm or village, a common element in English place-names: Berwick, Warwick. *Ceaster*, from *castra*, camp or fort, is a word that the English applied to any protected settlement, whether Roman or not, and Roman Deva, Isca, Glevum and Venta became Chester, Exeter, Gloucester and Winchester.

The first syllables of the last three names are ultimately Celtic, and the English accepted a number of British place-names, notably of rivers; Welsh *afon*, Cornish *avon*, means a river, *wy* or *gwy* means water, as in Wye; and Aire, Dee, Ouse, Severn, Tees, Thames and Trent are all Celtic, as are the names of some of the towns that stand on them: York and London, for example. Welsh *cwm* and Cornish *cum* became English *combe*, a low valley, as in Widecombe, Winchcombe, and *bre* is a hill, *dun* a hill-fort, as in the Bredon of Housman's poem. Most of the names in Wales and Cornwall are, of course, Celtic (Brythonic), many of them beginning with *pen*, summit, or *tre*, *tref*, homestead or town, or *llan*, *lan*, sacred enclosure. Perhaps the most musical group of names in the islands is that of four in mid-Cornwall near the upper River Fowey: Lanhydrock, Lostwithiel, Boconnoc, Restormel (*ros-tor-moel*, moor-hill-bare). It should be noted that, unlike English words, which generally have the accent on the first syllable, that of Celtic words is normally on the last but one: thus, Lanhȳdrock, in which the *hy* is pronounced *high*.

The English took very few Celtic words into their normal vocabulary from the fugitive and conquered Britons; *bin* may be one, and *brock*, badger, and *tor*, rocky peak, two more, though these they would find in place-names, such as modern Brockhurst and Dunster. Apart from these, and the few Latin words picked up from the British, and from the Romans themselves before their migration, the Anglo-Saxons spoke a purely Teutonic tongue; and such Old English remained for a 150 years, until the end of the sixth century.

The linguistic history of Gaul is a strange contrast to that of Britain. The Gallic Celts of what is now France accepted the

St Mark, from the *Lindisfarne Gospels c. 700*. With the spread of Christianity throughout England in the seventh century came learning and the art of writing.

The death of King Harold at Hastings, and beginning of the Norman conquest of England, 1066.

Latin speech of their Roman conquerors, and few traces of their Celtic language remain. Then, while the Anglo-Saxons were ravaging Roman Britain, their cousins, the equally destructive Teutonic tribes of the Franks, ravaged and conquered Roman Gaul, to which they gave their name, France. Yet, although equally contemptuous of Roman civilization, the Franks abandoned their native Teutonic speech for the Latin of the conquered romanized Gauls, from which modern French is derived. Across the Channel, therefore, the Teutonic-speaking English faced the Latin-speaking Teutons of France.

It must be remembered that the study of language is a recent phenomenon, that dictionaries and grammar books arc products of the last few hundred years. When the Indo-Europeans were forging their language, they did not think in terms of parts of speech, nouns and verbs, declensions and conjugations, but of a series of sounds so put together that they conveyed a meaning to others. Once a sound had become generally acceptable as meaning, for example, an action or experience, as for the Latins *audi* came to represent the experience of hearing, the problem was how to express such different meanings as I hear and You will hear. The obvious way was to modify the *audi* sound, so that it became *audio* and *audietis*, while *audiemur* represented We shall be heard. Similarly, as *puer* represented boy; *puero* meant To the boy; and *puerorum* Of the boys. Again, A good boy was *bonus puer*; Of a good boy *boni pueri*; but Of a good girl was *bonae puellae*; Of a good animal *boni animalis*. For there were three genders, masculine, feminine, neuter, and the adjective had to agree with its noun in gender as well as in number and case. Then, as there was no fixed order of words, a distinction had to be made between subject and object: *leonem audivit puer*, The boy has heard the lion, is very different from *puerum audivit leo*, The lion has heard the boy.

It was all very logical—up to a point—but immensely complex. Not only were there three genders, five declensions and four conjugations, but the formation of a speech before the invention of writing inevitably led to innumerable irregularities that had to be memorized. Gender, for example, had little or nothing to do with sex, but was grammatical, that is, masculine, feminine or neuter according to the word-ending. Thus, most nouns of the Third Declension ending in *-is* were feminine, but *sanguis, pulvis, cucumis* (*blood, dust, cucumber*) were perversely masculine. Then, the old Indo-European languages are complex because they are "synthetic": compressed, making additions to a root-sound do most of the work. Latin is a dead language, but if it were still a living tongue, it would, like its derivative French, have become simpler, less compressed, more "analytic": making use of auxiliary verbs, prepositions and a recognized word-order, instead of inflexions: Le garçon a entendu le lion. Le lion a entendu le garçon.

Modern German, though much less complex than Old High German, is still an inflected language. There are three genders, and these have little logical relation to sex: *das Bein*, the leg, is neuter, but *der Fuss*, foot, is masculine, and *die Hand* feminine. *Mann*, and *Knabe*, boy, are masculine, but *Weib, Mädchen, Kind*, wife, girl, child, are neuter. Nouns have four cases and varying declensions, each with its own set of inflexions to show number and case, and adjectives must agree with them in gender as well. The definite article has six forms, and a verb more than twice as many.

Old English resembled Modern German, but its grammar was even more complex. There was the same confusion of gender: *wif, mæden* and *cind* were neuter, and *wimman*, woman, was masculine. Nouns had four cases, and there were strong and weak declensions for stems ending in vowels or consonants. There was also a strong and weak declension of adjectives, which might assume ten or more forms: *glad*, for example:

SINGULAR	MASCULINE	FEMININE	NEUTER
NOM.	glæd	gladu	glæd
GEN.	glades	glædre	glades
DAT.	gladum	glædre	gladum
ACC.	glædne	glade	glæd
PLURAL			
NOM.	glade	glada	gladu
GEN.	glædra	glædra	glædra
DAT.	gladum	gladum	gladum
ACC.	glade	glada	gladu

Ranging from *se* to *ðara*, there were ten forms of the definite article, the single *the* of modern English. There was also a dual form for the personal pronoun: we two being *wit*, of you two *incer*.

There were more strong verbs than there are today; strong verbs forming their past tense by changing the vowel (*I give, gave*; *ic giefe, geaf*), weak verbs by adding *d* or *t* (*I live, lived*; *ic libbe, lifde*). There was no inflected future tense, which was generally represented by the present, though sometimes by *shall* or *will*, but the subjunctive mood was far more important and complex than it is today.

The heathen Anglo-Saxons were not a literate people, though they brought with them to Britain the knowledge of an alphabet that they had learned from their North Teutonic neighbours of Scandinavia. As most primitive peoples associate writing with magic, its letters were known as runes, secrets, mysteries; but like the Celtic oghams their use seems to have been confined to inscriptions, such as those on Northumbrian crosses, and with the re-introduction of Roman Christianity in the seventh century the English adopted the Roman alphabet. Their early writings were generally in Latin, like the version of the Lord's Prayer (Matthew vi. 9–13) in the Lindisfarne Gospels of *c.* 700:

> Pater noster, qui es in caelis, sanctificetur nomen tuum.
> Adveniat regnum tuum. Fiat voluntas tua sicut in caelo et in terra.
> Panem nostrum super-substantialem da nobis hodie.
> Et demitte nobis debita nostra sicut nos dimittimus debitoribus nostris.
> Et ne inducas nos in temptationem, sed libera nos a malo.

About the year 950 a priest added a literal translation in the Northumbrian dialect:

> Fader urer, ðu arð in heofnum, sie gehalgad noma ðin.
> To-cymeð ric ðin. Sie willo ðin suae is in heofne and in eorðo.
> Hlaf userne oferwistlic sel us to dæg.
> And forgef us scylda usra suae uoe forgefon scyldgum usum.
> And ne inlæd usih in costunge, ah gefrig usich from yfle.

Some 50 years later the Gospels were first translated into the West Saxon dialect:

> Fæder ure, þu þe eart on heofonum, si þin nama gehalgod.
> Tobecume þin rice. Gewurþe ðin willa on eorðan swa swa on heofonum.
> Urne gedæghwamlican hlaf syle us to dæg.
> And forgyf us ure gyltas swa swa we forgyfað urum gyltendum.
> And ne gelæd þu us on costnunge, ac alys us of yfele.

Finally, for comparison, here is the beginning of the German version of the prayer:

> Vater unser, der Du bist im Himmel, geheiliget werde Dein Name.
> Dein Reich komme. Dein Wille geschehe wie im Himmel also auch auf Erden. . . .

It is obvious that þ, the letter thorn, which the Anglo-Saxons took from their runic alphabet and added to the Roman, represents *th*, as does the crossed *d* (ð), an English invention. Strictly þ was the unvoiced *th* of *thin* (Greek θ), and ð the voiced *dh* of *then*, but this distinction was not always made in writing. The letters disappeared with the invention of printing, though Old English Þe is still to be found disguised as Ye in Ye Olde Englisshe this and that. It will be noted that, despite translation from Latin, no Latin word was taken into either the Northumbrian or Wessex version of the prayer. The sixteenth-century Prayer Book, however, has French-Latin *trespasses* for *scylda* and *gyltas* (*guilt*), *temptation* for *cost(n)unge*, and *deliver* for *gefrig* and *alys*. And two Old English words have replaced two older ones: *kingdom* for *rice* (German *Reich*) and *bread* for *hlaf* (*loaf*).

Old English pronunciation was broader and more guttural than its modern equivalent. All its letters were pronounced; thus, *cniht* (boy) had five sounds c-n-i-h-t, like German *Knecht* and *Knabe*, and unlike our modern *knight* and *knave*. A double consonant was pronounced twice, as in *swel-lan*, and a final *e* was always sounded.

Most consonants were pronounced much as they are today, though *c* was more often *k* (*boc*, book), and *sc* became *sh* (*scoh*, shoe; *fisc*, fish). Sometimes *g* was equal to *y*, as in *gyt*, yet; *dæg*, day. In the middle of a word, *f* might be *v*: *wulfas*, wolves, but *wulf*, wolf.

The main differences were in the vowels: approximately, *a* as in *father*; *æ* like *a* in *had*; *e* harsher than its modern sound; long *i* as in *machine* (the *i* of *fine* and *ow* of *town* were fifteenth-century inventions); short *u* as in *pull* and *Wuthering Heights*, not as in *sun*; *y* like French *u* (*mynster*, church).

This, then, was the *Englisc* spoken by the Anglo-Saxons who made themselves at home in their new country in the course of the sixth century: a highly inflected language with an almost purely Teutonic vocabulary. Its history since then, and this cannot be over-emphasized: its history since then has been mainly the simplification of its grammar by the dropping of inflexions, and the enrichment of its vocabulary by the adoption of foreign words.

5

CHRISTIANITY

THE DARK AGE of English history is the fifth and sixth centuries, the period between the withdrawal of the Romans in 410 and their return as Christian missionaries in 597. If any Anglo-Saxon scribes felt impelled to write a runic chronicle, their scripts have perished, and they have left no contemporary record of their conquest and settlement of Britain.

It is a period of mist and legend, when towards the end of the fifth century a romanized Briton, later called King Arthur, defended the Celtic West from the attacks of the heathen English; the period of another romanized Briton, St Patrick, who converted Ireland to Christianity, and inspired missionaries to visit other Celtic countries: Wales and western Scotland, Cornwall and Brittany. But in spite of missionaries, the Celts failed to unite, and remained a people of fiercely fighting tribes.

To begin with, too, the English were little more than tribal units fighting among themselves for the territory from which they had dispossessed the Britons, and the Saxons of Sussex, Middlesex and Essex, the Angles of Norfolk and Suffolk fought one another as fiercely as they fought the Celts. But the English were farmers as well as warriors and pirates, and in the course of the sixth century settled more peaceably to agriculture, and the three greater kingdoms of Northumbria, Mercia and Wessex began to emerge. There were differences of dialect, of course, in the English spoken within this wide region, by the Angles of the north and Midlands, Jutes of Kent, and Saxons of the south-west but, apart from a few inscriptions, we know little about their language before the seventh century.

It was now, after two centuries of barbarism, that isolated England was brought again into contact with Rome, with the new European civilization that was rising from the ruins of the

Christianity

old Empire. In the year 597 St Augustine, a monk sent by
Pope Gregory to refound the Church in England, landed in
Kent. It was a formidable task. The English had destroyed the
Romano-British churches, and their religion was that of Woden,
giver of victories, the god who welcomed the souls of warriors
to his palace of Valhalla, where he entertained them with the
fighting and feasting they had enjoyed while alive. Courage,
loyalty and fortitude in war were the great Teutonic virtues,
very different from the pacific humility and charity of Christian
ideals.

Nevertheless, Augustine converted Kent, and became the
first Archbishop of Canterbury. Forty years later Northumbria
was also converted, largely by the efforts of Aidan, a Celtic
missionary who founded a monastery on the island of
Lindisfarne, and by the end of the seventh century most of
England had accepted Christianity.

The impact of European civilization, a humane religion, and
an organized Church on the scarcely literate English had far-
reaching effects. Not only was it an introduction to a new
conception of morality and code of conduct, it was also an
introduction to writing and the Roman alphabet, to the Latin
version of the Bible and Latin literature. As a result, there was
a great flowering of learning and the arts in Northumbria in
the seventh and eighth centuries; churches and monasteries
were built, schools founded, sculptured crosses erected, and
the English began to write. Lindisfarne produced its beautiful
illuminated *Gospels*; Bede, in the monastery of Jarrow, wrote his
Ecclesiastical History of the English People, not in English but in
Latin, and told how Cædmon, an illiterate lay-brother, was
inspired by God to sing of the Creation. Other English poets
of the period were Cynewulf, who worked his name into his
verses in runic characters, and the unknown authors of "Deor",
"The Wanderer", and "The Ruin", in the last of which an
Englishman of the eighth century mourned the fallen towers
and walls of a city, possibly Bath, destroyed by his ancestors
some three centuries before:

> Beorht wæron burgræced, burnsele monige,
> heah horngestreon, heresweg micel,
> meodoheall monig, mandreama full.

55

(Bright were the town-dwellings, many the bath-halls, high the turrets, loud the warlike sound, many a mead-hall full of men's mirth.)

These English poets of the early Christian era still thought in terms of the heroic age of *Beowulf*, slayer of monsters, and hero of their national epic: of warriors and war, mead-hall and feast. Even Christ was an *ætheling*, princely heir to the throne and, like Woden, *sigora weard*, giver of victories. They also retained the old, inflated poetic diction, the "word-hoard", that differed from the ordinary language of speech and prose: *horngestreon* is literally horn-wealth, the soul is the breast-hoard, and arrows are *hilde-nædran*, war-adders. These conservative "lay-smiths" also retained the old conventions of verse, which was based, not on metre and rhyme, but on stress and alliteration: each line being divided into two parts, the first generally having two words beginning with the same letter, which is repeated in the second half.

By this time, the end of the eighth century, the ascendancy of Northumbria was passing to Wessex. But the ninth century was one of invasion and destruction, when the heathen Vikings of Scandinavia harried the land, destroying monasteries, libraries, and other cultural centres, so that the influence of the Church declined and learning decayed. So great was the devastation and loss that when Alfred the Great became King of Wessex in 871 he wrote:

Swa clæne hio wæs oðfeallenu on Angelkynne ðætte swiðe feawe wæron behionan Humbre þe hiora ðenunga cuðan understandan on Englisc, oððe furðum an ærendgewrit of Lædene on Englisc areccan; ond ic wene ðætte nauht monige begiondan Humbre næren. Swa feawe hiora wæron ðætte ic furðum anne anlepne ne mæg geðencean besuðan Temese ða ða ic to rice feng.

(So clean it [learning] was fallen away in England that very few there were on this side Humber who their service books could understand in English, or even a letter from Latin into English translate; and I ween that not many beyond Humber there were. So few of them there were that I even a single one may not think of south of Thames when I to the throne came.)

This comes from the Preface to Alfred's version of Pope Gregory's *Pastoral Care*, and Alfred, besides fighting the Danes, did his best to encourage the revival of learning by promoting the translation of other Latin works into English: among them Bede's *Ecclesiastical History of the English People* and Boethius' *Consolations of Philosophy*, and it may have been he who ordered the compilation of the *Anglo-Saxon Chronicle*. The early part of this, dealing with Roman Britain and the Anglo-Saxon invasion, is tradition rather than history, but from the ninth century until its last entry in 1154 it is a contemporary chronicle: the first history of a western nation to be written in its own language, not in Latin, and invaluable as a record, not only of events, sometimes in considerable detail, but also of the development of the English tongue. Alfred also brought over foreign scholars, and founded schools for the sons of noblemen in an attempt to repair the damage done by the Danes. He did not live to see the fruits of his labours, and it was only in the tenth century that learning returned to England with the monastic revival and teaching of Latin in schools.

One of these scholars was Aelfric "the grammarian", Abbot of Eynsham, who wrote a Latin conversation between a teacher and his pupils, remarkable as one of the first glimpses we have of English education. Either Aelfric or another added an English version, and in answer to the master's question one of his pupils replies: Ic eom geanwyrde munuc, and ic sincge ælce dæg seofon tida mid gebroþrum, and ic eom bysgod on rædinge and on sange; ac þeahhwæþere ic wolde betwenan leornian sprecan on Ledengereorde. (I am a professed monk, and I sing every day seven times with the brothers, and I am busy with reading and singing. But nevertheless, I should like betweenwhiles to learn to speak in the Latin tongue.) This was probably written in the early eleventh century, and it is significant that the passage contains two Latin words: *Leden* and *munuc*. Inevitably, in the course of the four centuries between the Christian and Norman conquest of England, a number of Latin words were taken into the language; but, as the scholars of the day were concerned with Roman Christianity, not with its pagan literature, most of these words related to the Church, its doctrine, organization and services: abbot, altar, candle, clerk, creed, devil, deacon, hymn, monk, minster (monastery), organ, priest, psalm. Obviously, few of these and similar ecclesiastical terms became part of everyday speech, but the names of trees, plants and herbs, some of them grown for medicinal purposes, would be more commonly used, and indicate both an increased knowledge of medicine and a more varied diet: beet, cherry, cole (cabbage), pea, pear, plant, plum, radish, rose.

Other Latin words taken into Old English referred to fishing, cooking, clothes, education, and some were names of animals, and diseases associated with animals: anchor, lobster, oyster, seine(-net); cook, cup, dish, fork, kettle, table; cap, mantle, pin, silk, sock; circle, master, school, verse; elephant, lion, mule, peacock, phoenix; cancer (crab), fever.

Before the Norman Conquest, the English had adopted more than 400 Latin words, most of them nouns, and this number does not include their derivatives. By the addition of prefixes and suffixes Old English could make numerous new words from the basic one, as, for example, derived from *king* we have *kinghood, kingless, kinglike, kingly, kingliness, kingdom, kingship*, and the verb *to king*. And the meaning of many of these can be reversed by the prefix *un-*. Then there are the compounds: *kingbolt, kingcraft, kingcup, kingfisher, kingpin, kingpost.* . . . Again, consider what can be done with the prefixes *be-, for-, fore-, mis-, over-, on-, to-, under-, with-*. Old English had many more verbs made with these prefixes than we have today. We still have *withdraw, withhold, withstand* (the first two are Middle English), but Old English had *withdrive, withspeak*, and some 50 more verbs in which *with* meant *against, away*, as it does in fight with, argue with.

However, in spite of borrowings, derivatives and compounds, the number of Latin words in everyday speech was not large. *Martyr, oflæte* (oblation), *tropere* (service-book) would rarely be heard outside church circles, and among the English peasants *lion, elephant* and *phoenix* would scarcely be household words. The English were conservative and, like their German cousins, preferred native words to foreign if they could be adapted and, if not, to coin new words to express new concepts. They did not need Latin words for *God, heofon, hel*, and preferred *Halig Gast* to *Spiritus Sanctus, Ut-færeld* to *Exodus, godspell* (good tidings) to *evangelium, lufu* to *charity, wundor* to *miracle*, withering *genitherung* to *damnation*, *eorþ-gemet* to *geometry*, *tungol-æ* (star-lore) to *astronomy*, *hærfest* (harvest) to *autumn*. And in Aelfric's *Colloquy*, although the Latin *prime* and *nones* are accepted as two of the canonical "hours", the others are rendered *uhtsang* (matins), *undertid* (tierce), *middæg* (sext), *æfen-sange* (evensong, vespers), *niht-sange* (compline).

If, therefore, the number of Latin words, particularly those in common use, was relatively small before the Norman Conquest, Old English had been greatly enriched by the development of its ability to make new native words that were the equivalents of foreign ones.

But before the Normans came, the language had been further modified by an earlier invasion of Northmen.

6

THE VIKINGS

IN THE YEAR 787 the *Anglo-Saxon Chronicle* recorded a coastal raid
by three foreign ships, and added, "Þæt wæron þa ærestan scipu
Deniscra monna þe Angelcynnes lond gesohton". (They were
the first ships of Danish men to visit the land of the English.)

The Danes were Scandinavians who had exchanged their
native Norway for the country vacated by the Angles and Jutes
when they occupied Britain, thus giving it the name of Denmark. Their raid was a fragment of the eighth-century
Scandinavian, or Viking, explosion, when the Swedes burst
into Russia, and the Norsemen of Norway sailed plundering
round the north of Scotland, where some of them settled, while
others occupied the western coast as far south as Lancashire,
and even part of south Wales. They also occupied Ireland and
the Isle of Man, and conquered the Frankish province to which
they gave their name, Normandy.

Swedes, Norsemen and Danes were all members of the North
Teutonic stock, nearly related, therefore, to the English, and
speaking similar languages. Of these tall, fair warriors, the
Norsemen sailed as far west and east as North America and the
Levant, but the Danes concentrated on the easier plunder of
eastern England.

To begin with, they confined their marauding to swift coastal
raids, such as those on Lindisfarne and Bede's old monastery
of Jarrow, but for 851 the *Anglo-Saxon Chronicle* has the ominous
entry: "Hæþne men ærest ofer winter sæton". (Heathen men for
the first time remained over winter.) Raids now became
invasion; London and Canterbury were sacked, and by 876
the Danes had conquered Northumbria, and were "ploughing
and making a living for themselves". Then, after seizing East
Anglia, they advanced on Wessex, but were defeated by Alfred
at Ethandun, and by the Treaty of Wedmore, 878, they agreed

60

The Vikings

to accept Christianity and retire into the Danelaw, the country east of Watling Street, the Roman road that ran from London to Chester.

Although there was more fighting, as at Brunanburh, an English victory celebrated in a famous poem, the tenth century was on the whole one of reconstruction, when Alfred's successors reasserted their authority over the Danelaw, and English and Danes learned to live and work together. They even fought together against fresh hordes of Norse and Danish invaders at the end of the century, and died together at the Battle of Maldon, 991, a defeat described in another fine English poem. The attempt of Ethelred the Unready (without *rede*, or counsel) to buy off the invaders with Danegeld proved futile; in 1016 Canute seized his throne, and until 1042 England was ruled by Danish kings.

By that time most of the Danes had lived peaceably and inter-married with the English for 150 years in the north and east of England, time for five or six generations to grow up and become one people. There had been little language difficulty to prevent or retard the mixture of the two peoples, for it would not take them long to learn to understand their nearly related tongues. There were differences, however, between their West and North Teutonic languages, differences of inflexion and pronunciation as well as of vocabulary, and inevitably Old English was modified by the Scandinavian tongue of the newcomers.

One of the main differences lay in the fondness of the Scandinavians for the gutturals *k* and *g*. Thus, they retained the original Teutonic *sk* sound, whereas the English had modi-fied it to the softer *sh*, which they wrote *sc*. The Scandinavians, therefore, said *skor, skel, skip, fiskr, diskr*, which the English wrote *scoh, sciell, scip, fisc, disc*, and pronounced *shoe, shell, ship, fish, dish*. They did not adopt the Scandinavian pronunciation of any of these, and retained their own word *scyrte* (shirt), transforming Norse *skyrta* into a woman's dress, *skirt*. (Even today many English people prefer to change Norwegian *ski* to *shi*.) On the other hand, they did abandon the *y* pronuncia-tion of *g* in the important word *give*, and eventually changed the *y* sound of *æg* into the Norse *egg*, though they kept their own pronunciation of *dæg* (day).

61

Many borrowed Scandinavian words, therefore, can be distinguished by the initial *sk* or hard *sc*, and hard *g* before *e* and *i*: scalp, scare, scarf, scold, scowl; skill, skin, skip, skulk, sky; gear, geld, gift, gill, girth. And there are many other words in which the gutturals are prominent: call, cast, clip, crave, crook; keel, kid, kilt, kindle, k-nife; gap, gape, gasp, gate, get, glitter; bracken, dike, freckle, link, take.

Although these are all characteristic, borrowings were by no means confined to such words, nor were many of them new in the sense that they represented anything unknown to the English. The Vikings were a primitive people and, unlike the learned latinisms that the English were absorbing at the same time, their words concerned everyday things, many of them being merely variants of, or substitutes for, English ones. Thus, the simpler Norse *systir* (sister) was preferred to English *sweoster* (German *Schwester*); and Norse *leg* replaced English *sceanca* (shank), which was reduced to the lower half of the limb. *Sky* supplanted English *wolcen*, though it has survived in the form of *welkin*; and if *vindauga* (wind-eye) had not replaced English *eagþyrl* (eye-hole) we might have had, on the analogy of *nosþyrl* (nostril), *eyetril* for *window*.* Then, *tacan* (take) eventually replaced *niman* (German *nehmen*), though Chaucer used the form *nome* ("Hir eem [uncle] anoon in armes hath hir nome"), and Shakespeare had his Corporal Nym, one of his pickers-up of unconsidered trifles.

There was one class of word, however, that was a real innovation: that dealing with legal and political affairs. *Law* itself is Scandinavian, as is *outlaw*; and *thriding*, or *riding*, was one of the three parts that came to be combined into Yorkshire. Most of the other legal terms of the Norsemen were superseded by those of their Norman cousins, even greater sticklers for law and orderly administration than the Viking invaders of England.

Scandinavian words did not all gain immediate currency and, as the original changes took place almost entirely in the Danelaw, it was some time before they were accepted in the south and west, if ever they were accepted. For when standard English came to be that of London, thousands of Danish and

* Camden, in the early days of etymology, ingeniously derived *window* from *windor*, "a doore against the winde".

Norse words were left stranded as part of northern dialect: such words as *beck* (brook), *gate* (street), *ghyll* (ravine, deep hole), *lake* (to play, be unemployed). But at least a thousand have become a part of standard English; most important of all, perhaps, because so frequently used, are the pronouns *they*, *their*, *them*, instead of Old English *hie*, *hiera*, *him*, and the plural form *are* instead of *syndon*, of the verb *to be*. Whenever we say 'they are' we are speaking Norse rather than English: a measure of the linguistic importance of the Scandinavian invasion.

This is commemorated in its place-names. As soon as the traveller along the Fosse Way crosses Watling Street from the south-west, he leaves behind the country of Saxon *hams* and *tons*, and enters one of Danish *bys*: Blaby, Enderby, Oadby, Thurnby. These are now suburbs of Leicester, once, like Derby, a Danish garrison town and trading centre. The Danes, unlike the English, were town-dwellers, and *by* (*byr*, town, village) is probably the origin of *by-law*, both Danish words. Nearly a half of the 1,500 Scandinavian place-names end in *-by*, from Rugby to Whitby, Maltby to Spilsby, east of Lincoln, a Celtic-Roman name (Lyn-colonia, Lake-colony), but another of the Danish "five towns", round which there are scores of *-bys*. Here also are Sausthorpe (Sheep-village) and Hogsthorpe, Bratoft and Fishtoft; and *thorp* (village) and *toft* (homestead) are two more of the commonest Scandinavian terminations. Those with *-by* are characteristically Danish, and are commonest in Lincolnshire and Yorkshire, each of which has some 300 Danish place-names, and Leicestershire has another hundred.

Another common name is *thwaite* (paddock), but this is characteristic of the Norwegian settlements in Cumberland and Westmorland, each with about a hundred Scandinavian names. Applethwaite was a piece of land owned by Wordsworth, at the head of Bassenthwaite, near Braithwaite. Other Scandinavian names in the Lake District are *beck* (Starbeck, Trout-beck); *gill*, *ghyll* (Wordsworth's Greenhead Ghyll); *fell*, mountain (Rydal Fell, Scafell).

Here we return to the familiar Scandinavian *sk*, and if we move into North Yorkshire, crossing Scales Moor, we come to the silvery-grey limestone *scars*: to Gordale Scar, and Gaping Ghyll on Pen-y-ghent, a Norse pot-hole on a Celtic mountain. And so to Skipton (a scandinavianized form of English Shipton,

which it would have been on the other side of Watling
Street), to Scunthorpe and Skegness on the Lincolnshire coast.
Tennyson was a Lincolnshire man, as we might tell from his
poetry, in which he celebrated his native thorps and garths;
garth being another Scandinavian name for Old English (and
present-day American) *yard*, meaning *garden*, a variation that
came in with the Normans.

There are, of course, Scandinavian place-names south-west
of Watling Street; there are garths in Wales, and on the
Pembrokeshire coast is the isolated Tenby, legacy of the
Norsemen who settled there a thousand years ago. Then, in
Canute's reign a few Danes acquired land in Wessex, but their
place-names become rarer towards the far west. Devon has a
few, but Cornwall none.

There seem to have been no hereditary surnames in England
before the Norman Conquest; like his horse or dog, a man had
only one name, though he might be distinguished from others
by the name of his dwelling (Northwood), or his occupation
(Shepherd), or by a nick-name (an eke-name or also-name),
and one or the other might come to name a place. Thus, English
Tatsfield is the "Field of Tatel", and Danish Spilsby the
"Village of Spilli (the Waster)". In Lincolnshire and the north
of England before the Conquest, there were probably as many
people with Scandinavian as with English names, many of
them associated with places. Places remain while families
disperse, yet even today a northern directory has far more
names of Scandinavian origin than a southern one: Storey
(strong), Skegg (bearded), Scarr (hare-lipped), Corby, Kirkby,
Slingsby, Kettle, Thurkell.

Although the Vikings destroyed the flourishing culture of
Northumbria, and had little to offer in exchange, the beneficial
effect of their invasion and settlement on the development of
the English language was immense. First: because Old English
and Old Norse were so nearly related, their words so easily
interchanged, the English people became accustomed to
borrowing any number of quite ordinary words, unlike those
selected from Latin by scholars, so preparing the way for
wholesale borrowing from languages less closely related. Again:
because so many of their words were nearly the same, though
differing in detail, in converse English and Dane would concen-

The Tower of London: the Norman White Tower, *c.* 1085, symbol of English subjection to Norman rule, and of the English language to Norman-French.

Gloucester Cathedral Chancel, rebuilt *c.* 1350 when Chaucer was a boy. English Perpendicular Gothic breaks away from French Flamboyant, its tracery even applied to the original Norman walls. Symbol of the emergence of the English language from Norman-French subjection.

The Vikings

trate on essentials and neglect detail, as does the inexperienced traveller today when trying to make himself understood abroad; a verb, a noun and a gesture will suffice, and gender and inflexions can be ignored. While in Wessex, therefore, they still observed the complexities of English grammar, adding *-an* or *-e* or *-s* to form a genitive singular, in Northumbria they began to form any genitive with *-s*, and to ignore the niceties of grammatical gender and declension. Thanks largely to the Vikings, therefore, some of the unnecessary elaboration of Old English grammar was abandoned, and the historic process of simplification began.

7

THE NORMANS
1066–1150

DANISH RULE IN England ended with the death of Canute's
second son in 1042, when the exiled English king, Edward the
Confessor, was restored to the throne. Then, when he died
childless early in 1066 the Witan elected his brother-in-law,
Harold Earl of Wessex, to succeed him. But Edward's cousin,
William Duke of Normandy, maintaining that he had a better
claim to the crown, invaded England, and at Hastings defeated
Harold, who was killed in the battle. The Normans occupied
London, and on Christmas Day 1066 the Conqueror was
crowned William I of England.

It is important to bear in mind who the Normans were.
Gaul (France), like Britain, had been occupied by the Celts in
prehistoric times, and both countries had been conquered by
the Romans; but whereas Latin did not replace the Celtic
speech of the British, it almost entirely supplanted that of the
Gauls. Then came the Teutonic invasions: of Britain by the
Anglo-Saxons, of Gaul by the Franks, each people giving its
name to the conquered country: England and France. But
there the resemblance ended; the English took very little,
either Celtic or Latin, from the speech of the romanized Britons,
but the Franks adopted the Latin dialect of the conquered
Gauls. Next came the Viking invasions, and as Alfred sur-
rendered the Danelaw to the Danes, so the French king sur-
rendered the province of Neutria to the Norsemen, who gave it
their name, Normandy. Yet, even though Danish kings ruled
England for nearly thirty years, nowhere, not even in
Northumbria, did their language supplant English; but by the
beginning of the eleventh century the Normans were speaking
French, the Romance language of the Franks, which they had
taken from the Gauls, who had had it from the Romans.

The Normans

In 1066, therefore, when the Normans conquered England, the Teutonic language that had been spoken there for six centuries with comparatively little change, had to compete with a Romance language, descended from the Romans, which had been adopted by three peoples, and outlived two conquests. And French was the simpler, the original synthetic Latin having been transformed by its borrowers, Celts, Teutons and Scandinavians, into a simpler analytic language. If English had remained the highly inflected Teutonic tongue that it was, there can be little doubt that it would have succumbed to its rival. Yet it was English that was to survive this conquest, though an English transformed, almost transfigured.

The Normans were nothing if not thorough, and their conquest was a real one. William distributed the estates of the English nobility among his followers, who were responsible to him for the government of the country, and he appointed others to govern the Church, from archbishops to the abbots of monasteries. Rebellion was ruthlessly crushed, Yorkshire laid waste, and their castles remain to show how the English were kept in subjection. And the Anglo-Saxon chronicler recorded how they "worhton castelas wide geond þas þeode, and earm folc swencte; and a syððan hit yflade swiðe. Wurðe god se ende þonne God wylle". (built castles widely throughout the land, and poor people oppressed; and ever since it has grown greatly in evil. May the end be good when God will.)

As William was Duke of Normandy as well as King of England, and his nobles held land in both countries, they naturally thought of themselves as Normans, not English: a conquering caste distinguished from their subjects by their speech. French was the sign of a superior people, as English was to become in the days of the British Empire. But, as it was also a status symbol, it was not long before the English upper and educated classes began to learn the language, and by the twelfth century England was divided socially into the few who spoke French and the many who could speak only English.

English, therefore, was reduced to little more than the speech of illiterate serfs, and as the early Normans made little attempt to learn the language, comparatively few French words found their way into ordinary speech during the first century after the Conquest. These were mainly such as a servant would have to know: *servant* itself and *message*, and *dinner*, and perhaps it was now that the animals kept by these humble folk, the English ox, calf, sheep and pig, began to be transformed into the French beef, veal, mutton and pork that they dressed for their masters' tables.

If to begin with, however, French had little effect on the English vocabulary, indirectly it had a momentous effect on the grammar. Simplification had begun in Northumbria, where the peaceful intercourse of English and Danes had led to the dropping of inflexions, and now that English was the normal speech of few but peasants, the process was accelerated. Such people could not be expected to wrestle with the elaborate complexities of Old English, and they began to drop the case-endings of nouns, reducing them to a vestigial final -*e*, apart from the genitive, which they distinguished by -*s*. In the northern and midland dialects the plural, too, became -*s* or -*es*, though in the south -*en* was favoured for a long time: *lambren* (like *oxen*) and *eyren* for lambs and eggs. Pronouns lost many of their inflexions, adjectives all, and the ten forms of the definite article were reduced to a simple *the*. Verbs, too, were simplified by the shedding of inflexions (though we still add an unnecessary -*s* to the third person singular, present tense, *he gives* but *he gave*), and many strong, or irregular, verbs became weak, forming the past tense and participle by the addition of a uniform -*ed*, instead of changing the vowel: *help, helped, have helped*, instead of *help, holp, holpen*.

The loss of inflexion of noun and adjective made grammatical gender meaningless, and commonsense, natural gender replaced the old artificial one; living things were masculine or feminine according to sex, and other things neuter; *wife* became feminine instead of neuter, *door* neuter instead of feminine. Then, the change from an inflected to an uninflected, from a synthetic to an analytic, language, necessitated a recognized word order (subject-verb-object), and the extended use of prepositions to indicate the relation of words: *of words* for worda, *to these words* for þissum wordum.

Of course, all these changes did not come about at once, but were spread over a period of some four centuries, but how far they had gone by 1154, a hundred years after the Conquest, may be judged from the last entry in the *Anglo-Saxon Chronicle*, recording the death of Stephen and accession of Henry II:

On þis gear wærd þe king Steph. ded and bebyried þer his wif and his sune wæron bebyried æt Fauresfeld, þæt minstre hi makeden. Þa þe king was ded, þa was þc corl beionde sæ, and ne durste nan man don oþer bute god for þe micel eie of him. Þa he to Engleland com, þa was he underfangen mid micel wurtscipe, and to king bletcæd in Lundene on þe Sunnendæi beforen midwinterdæi, and held þær micel curt.

This is clearly much closer to modern English than Alfred's version of the *Pastoral Care* (p. 56), written nearly three centuries earlier, and a literal translation shows how close it is:

In this year was the king Stephen dead and buried where his wife and his son were buried at Faversham, the monastery they made [founded]. When the king was dead, then was the earl beyond sea, and durst no man do other but good for the great awe of him. When he to England came, then was he received with great worship, and to king blessed [consecrated] in London on the Sunday before midwinter day, and held there great court.

There is only one French word in the passage: *court*, characteristically a word of social distinction. But there are only two words no longer in use: *wærd*, worth in the sense of became, was, and *underfangen*; and there are fourteen that are the same in both versions: *this—the king—and—his—was—man—other—for—of him—he—to—in—on—held*. Most of the old inflexions have been dropped: *on þis gear* instead of *on þissum geare* (we say 'in this year' though 'on this day'); *micel* instead of *miclan* and *miclum*; and *þe* (the) is used throughout: *for þe, on þe*, instead of *þam*.

It is true that this version of the *Chronicle* was written at Peterborough in the East Midland dialect, and that the southern dialect was more conservative, but as modern English is descended from the East Midland, it can be said that by 1150 the Old English period was over and another beginning: that of Middle English, which was to last until about 1500, making the transition from the old to the new.

8

MIDDLE ENGLISH
1150–1500

By the beginning of the thirteenth century, the period of King John and Magna Carta, after five or six generations of intermarriage, the distinction between Norman and English had disappeared. Many of the better educated could now speak English as well as French, and the clergy also spoke Latin, but French still remained a sign of social superiority and the speech of the upper classes, while English was little more than that of illiterate peasants, the vast majority.

Although the connection with France was weakened by John's loss of Normandy in 1204, after which the nobility had either to relinquish their Norman estates or go to live on them, it was not severed. For John had inherited the French provinces of his father Henry II, Anjou and Maine, and of his mother Eleanor of Aquitaine. These were in turn inherited by his son Henry III, whose mother and wife were both French, so that during his long reign (1216–72) England was governed, or misgoverned, by his foreign favourites and relations from central and southern France. As this was the period when French was recognized as the principal literary language of Europe, the influence of France on England was immense, and French remained the fashionable speech.

By the middle of the century, however, English had been so simplified by its humble speakers that the upper classes were becoming bilingual, and inevitably, when they tried to make themselves understood in the vulgar tongue, they substituted French words for the English ones they did not know. In this way began the flow of French words into English which, to the inestimable enrichment of the language, was to swell into a torrent in the age of Chaucer. Yet, as Robert of Gloucester wrote about 1300, "Vor bote a man conne Frenss, men telþ of him lute": (For but a man know French, men account little of him). And some twenty years later Ralph Higden, in his Latin *Polychronicon*, noted how schoolchildren were taught their lessons in French, and how the socially ambitious tried to learn the language.

At the same time, there were protests against this tyranny of French, notably by the author of *Cursor Mundi*, a sort of world history:

> Þis ilk bok it es translate
> In to Inglis tong to rede
> For þe loue of Inglis lede [folk],
> Inglis lede of Ingland,
> For þe commun at [to] understand.
> Frankis rimes here I redd
> Communlik in ilka sted;
> Mast es it wroght for frankis man,
> Quat is for him na frankis can?
> Of Ingland þe nacion
> Es Inglis man þar in commun;
> Þe speche þat man wit mast may spede
> Mast þarwit to speke war nede.
> Selden was for ani chance
> Praised Inglis tong in france;
> Giue we ilkan þare langage,
> Me þink we do þam non outrage.

Ironically enough, this appeal for English for the English, written about 1300, in the northern (probably Lincolnshire) dialect, contains eight French words: *common, rimes, commonly, nation, chance, praised, language, outrage,* as well as the Latin *translate*.

The fourteenth century was to be one of great change. From the time of the Conquest and submergence of the English language, there had been no literature of any importance, for few of its speakers could read; but by 1300, with the growth of the woollen industry and towns, a new English-speaking middle class was emerging. The craftsmen organized themselves in gilds, and it was for performance by the gildsmen of York, Chester, Coventry and Wakefield that, about 1340, miracle plays were written in English, the dramatic equivalents of the Bible stories portrayed in the stained-glass windows of their churches.

By this time the Hundred Years War with France had begun. Edward III, whose long reign (1327–77) covered the middle half of the century, was a devotee of chivalry and war, and his brilliant victory at Crécy in 1346 so roused anti-French feeling and a spirit of nationalism in the English that the speaking of French became, if not unpatriotic, at least less fashionable, and as French speakers turned more and more to English, more and more French words poured into the language.

Then in 1348–49 came the disaster of the Black Death, the great plague or, to use the French word, *murrain*, which killed almost half the people of England. As a result, there was an acute shortage of labour, peasants were able to extort their freedom from feudal servitude, and a new class of independent land-workers arose, some of whom were soon to become yeomen with small farms of their own.

After 1350, therefore, the condition of England, and of the English language, was very different from what it had been in 1300, and that it was so is testified by the translator of *Polychronicon* in 1385. Referring to Higden's account of the teaching of schoolchildren in French, he added the note:

Þys manere was moche y-used tofore þe furste moreyn, and ys siþþe somdel ychaunged. For Iohan Cornwel, a mayster of gramere, chayngede þe lore in gramerscole and construccion of Freynsch into Englysch . . . so þat now . . . in al þe gramerscoles of Engelond childern leveþ Frensch and construeþ and lurneþ an Englysch . . . þat now childern of gramerscole conneþ no more Frensch þan can here lift heele . . . Also gentil men habbeþ now moche yleft for to teche here childern Frensch.

By 1385, then, French was no longer the medium of teaching in schools, nor was it the language normally spoken by gentlemen. Nor was it any longer the language of the Law Courts, for a statute of 1362 decreed that, as French was so little known, all pleas should be made and judged in the English tongue, and recorded in Latin. French indeed, or rather Anglo-French, was something of a joke, as we know from Chaucer's description of the Prioress in his *Canterbury Tales*:

> And Frenssh she spak ful faire and fetisly,
> After the scole of Stratford atte Bowe,
> For Frenssh of Parys was to hire unknowe.

The lingo picked up in an English nunnery by this affected lady bore little resemblance to real French. And Chaucer knew, for he was one of the most travelled men of his age.

It is scarcely surprising that modern English literature should begin in the second half of the fourteenth century when, after three centuries of subjection, the language re-emerged as that of the whole nation. But it was very different from that spoken by the English before the Conquest, as can be seen by comparing King Alfred's version of Boethius with Chaucer's:

> Hu gesælig seo forme eld was þises midangeardes, ða ælcum men þuhte genog on pære eorþan wæstmum . . . Ealne weg hi slepon ute on triowa sceadum; hluterra wella wæter hi druncon.

> Blisful was the firste age of men. They heelden hem apayed with the metes that the trewe feeldes broughten forth . . . They slepen holsome slepes uppon the gras, and dronken of the rennynge watres.

But Chaucer was no great master of prose, and far more illuminating is the latest poetry of his *Canterbury Tales*, begun, perhaps, in April 1387:

> Whan that Aprill with his shoures soote
> The droghte of March hath perced to the roote,
> And bathed every veyne in swich licour
> Of which vertu engendred is the flour:
> Whan Zephirus eek with his sweete breeth
> Inspired hath in every holt and heeth
> The tendre croppes, and the yonge sonne
> Hath in the Ram his halve cours yronne,
> And smale foweles maken melodye,

73

That slepen al the nyght with open ye
(So priketh hem nature in hir corages):
Thanne longen folk to goon on pilgrimages,
And palmeres for to seken straunge strondes,
To ferne halwes, kowthe in sondry londes;
And specially from every shires ende
Of Engelond to Caunterbury they wende,
The hooly blisful martir for to seke,
That hem hath holpen whan that they were seeke.

The old grammatical genders, and inflexions of noun and adjective have gone, and all that remains is a final *-e*, and an *-es* to denote the plural (*shoures soote*) and genitive (*shires ende*). Although *hem*, *hir* and *his* still stand for modern *them*, *their*, *its*, the definite article is always a uniform *the*. Apart from a few now obsolete words (*halwes*—shrines), and infinitives and present tense plurals in *-n* (*to goon*, *sleepen*), there is little save spelling (and pronunciation) to distinguish Chaucer's language from our own. Its grammar had been wonderfully simplified by generations of uneducated peasants, and now that it had emerged again as the speech of educated people, and the medium of poets, all things were possible.

Then, there is the vocabulary. In these eighteen lines, one word in seven is French, from the noun *April* to the adverb *specially*, a French adjective, *especial*, adverbalized by the Old English suffix *-ly*. (*Martyr* was taken direct from Latin in the early days of English Christianity.) Most of them are nouns, typically abstract disyllables (*virtue*, *nature*), but there are two adjectives (*tender*, *strange*) and three verbs (*pierce*, *engender*, *inspire*). And these syllabled abstractions (*melody*, *pilgrimages*) contrast and combine with the short English concrete nouns (*holt*, *heath*) to make a new music. The basic vocabulary is essentially that of the Anglo-Saxons who had invaded Britain a thousand years before, but it is now a simple analytic language instead of a complex synthetic one, and its ancient Teutonic "word-hoard" has been immensely enriched by the adoption of thousands of French words that come ultimately from Latin.

More than 10,000 of these words came into the language during the Middle English period, and most of them are still in use, as can be seen by turning the pages of a dictionary: *abandon, abase, abash, abate* ... *bachelor, bacon, baggage, bail* ... *cabin, cadence, cage, calamity* ... As the Normans were efficient administrators, soldiers, churchmen and builders, and as for three centuries the law had been conducted in French, many of the adopted words refer to government, war, religion and legal affairs, and there are innumerable words descriptive of the life and pleasures of an upper class, and their interest in the arts, as a few examples will suggest:

Government, city, constable, counsel, county, mayor, parliament, revenue, statute, tax.

War, army, battle, captain, fortress, garrison, navy, siege, soldier, vanquish.

Religion, baptise, bible, miracle, penitence, pray, preach, saint, sermon, vicar.

Justice, arrest, crime, jury, legacy, prison, punish, property, tenant, trespass.

Pleasure, fashion, feast, gown, jewel, leisure, luxury, mansion, satin, tennis.

Art, arch, chant, comedy, music, paint, poetry, prose, rime (rhyme), statue.

Of course there were losses when French drove English words out of use, though generally speaking it was things of secondary importance that changed, while fundamentals remained. Thus *eam* became *uncle*, and *aunt, nephew, niece, cousin* are French, but *father, mother, brother, sister* are Old English. So too are *king* and *queen, lady* (*hlæfdige*—loaf-kneader) and *lord* (loaf-ward), but the splendid *atheling* declined into the hybrid *noble-man* and, apart from *earl* and *knight*, other aristocratic titles from *duke* to *baron* became French. French, too, at the other end of the social scale, were the barber, butcher, carpenter, grocer and tailor. The months also changed names, Wulfmonath (Wolfmonth) to January, Wintermonath or Helighmonath (Holymonth) to December, while Hegmonath (Haymonth) became July which, commemorating Julius Caesar, should be pronounced to rhyme with duly, as it did until the eighteenth century. The days of the week, however, except Satur(n's)day, remained English, as did *day, week, month, year* and *time* itself, though *century* is French as are at the other extreme, *hour, minute, second* (secondary minute). Most of the parts of the body are English (*face* and *stomach* are exceptions), a fact that Shakespeare turned into comedy in *Henry V*, when Alice teaches Princess Katharine of France to say "de hand, de fingres, de mails, de arm, de bilbow, de nick, de foot, et de sin".

Then, although many Old English words were lost, others remained alongside their French equivalents:

book—volume	far—distant	ask—question
room—chamber	greedy—covetous	begin—commence
sorrow—grief	holy—sacred	end—finish
smell—scent	red—scarlet	find—discover
tale—story	small—petty	teach—instruct
work—labour	thin—meagre	understand—comprehend

Such synonyms, however, have generally developed slightly different meanings, which is another reason why English is so rich in words and subtle distinctions. "Within the book and volume of my brain," says Hamlet, recognizing the greater bulk of volume; one would not engage a chamber at an hotel; *scent* is politer than *smell*, much politer than *stench*, *stink*; and how much better is "In the beginning was the word," than In the commencement.

Another source of synonyms, or near-synonyms, was the borrowing of French words from different regions: first from Normandy, then from Central France. As these dialects differed, the same word was sometimes adopted in two forms, with more or less different meanings. Examples of such doublets are: *catch—chase*; *cattle—chattel*; *gaol—jail*; *launch—lance*; *wage—gage*; *warden—guardian*.

This adoption of Latin words by way of French naturally encouraged their direct adoption, and in the fourteenth and fifteenth centuries hundreds of Latin words were added to the French influx, chiefly from literary sources, *literary* itself being one of them. German, never having been subject to French influence like English, has resisted borrowings from Latin, but by 1500 the English vocabulary of noun and adjective, verb and adverb, was already becoming almost as much Latin as Teutonic. But it was not only words that were added, it was also variety; variety of movement, as foreign polysyllables extended the language's rhythmical resources; variety of sound, as French-Latin terminations alternated and mingled with English endings:

free-dom	liber-ty	duke-dom
kind-ness	benevol-ence	easi-ness
hope-less	desper-ate	spirit-less
wonder-ful	admir-able	peace-ful
man-hood	cour-age	stopp-age
ful-some	excess-ive	talk-ative
wash-ing	laund-ry	wash-able
hard-ship	priv-ation	better-ment

In the first column both root and suffix are English; in the second both are French; in the third the first four words illustrate the way in which a French root was given an English suffix, the last four the reverse process of attaching a French suffix to an English root. Hybrid words became common: *peace-maker*, *grand-father*, a version of the French *grand-sire*, but *grand-son* is an English invention. French *re-* (again) could be prefixed to English verbs: *re-build*, *re-make*; and the negative prefixes, English *un-* and French *dis-*, could be added to words of either origin: *un-dress*, *dis-own*, *un-arm*, *dis-arm*. (A recent solecism is the confusion of *disinterested*, meaning impartial, with *uninterested*.)

Of course, the adoption and absorption of all such words and their derivatives was a lengthy process, and when Chaucer was writing it was not easy to say exactly what was the English language, as he himself ruefully observed in his Envoy to *Troilus and Criseyde*: "ther is so gret diversite / In Englissh and in writyng of oure tonge". And at about the same time the translator of *Polychronicon* described how the mixing of the English with Danes and Normans had so confounded the native tongue that "som useþ strange wlaffyng, chyteryng, harryng and garryng grisbittyng".

Men of þe est wiþ men of þe west, as hyt were undur þe same party of heuene, accordeþ more in sounyng of speche þan men of þe norþ wiþ men of þe souþ. Þerfore hyt ys þat Mercij, þat buþ [beeth] men of myddel Engelond, as hyt were parteners of þe endes, undurstondeþ betre þe syde

77

longages, norþeron and souþeron, þan norþeron and souþeron understondeþ eyþer oþer. Al þe longage of þe Norþumbres, and specialych at York, ys so scharp, slyttyng and frotyng and unschape þat we souþeron men may þat longage unneþe [scarcely] undurstonde.

The northern and southern dialects sounded almost like different languages, the one with its harsh scandinavianisms, the other with its buzzing *v*'s and *z*'s "vrom Zomerzet". The East and West Midland dialects were a compromise,* and it was partly for this reason that one of them was to become the standard speech of England. There could be little doubt as to which would triumph, for the East Midland was the speech of London, the seat of government and great commercial centre, and it is from Chaucer's East Midland dialect that standard English has evolved.

Although the language of Chaucer is fairly easy to read today, at least much easier than King Alfred's, it would be barely intelligible if Chaucer himself were to read it aloud. As might be expected there was a mixture of Teutonic and French elements in its pronunciation. Thus, though four of the short vowels were much the same as in modern English, *u* was pronounced as in *full* (and German *um*), and the final *e* of a word as *e* in *Knabe* and *a* in *sofa*. Most of the consonants, too, were as in modern English, but all were pronounced, and *gh* was like *ch* in *loch*: *light* like German *Li-ch-t*. The greatest differences were in the long vowels: *age* and *fine*, for example, having the *ah* and *ee* sound of the French words, for there was still no modern long *i*; the *e* of sweet that of *é* in *été* or *a* in *late*, *e* of *breeth, heeth* (*breath, heath*) having the sound of *air*; and in some words long *o* was pronounced *aw*: *go* (gaw), *foe* (faw).

After the brief successes of Henry V's reign (1413–22), the fifteenth century was one of dreary defeat by the French in the last half of the Hundred Years War, followed by 30 years of civil war, the Wars of the Roses; but all through these unhappy times the East Midland dialect was asserting its pre-eminence both in speech and writing; and when, in 1476, William Caxton

---

* Even today northern and southern speech mingle in the Midlands: in the region of Lichfield, for example, birthplace of Dr Johnson, for whom *punch* was *poonsh*, and *there* was *theer*.

set up his printing-press in Westminster, its position was assured. The Middle English period, like the Middle Ages, was over, and so was the connection with France, which had begun 400 years before with the Norman Conquest.

9

TUDOR TRANSITION
1485–1603

THE EUROPE OF 1500 was very different from that of 1450. The Renaissance was nearing its climax in Italy, where architects, sculptors and painters had returned to classical forms and themes; the scholars of Constantinople were fleeing west from the conquering Turks, bringing with them their knowledge of Greek; Columbus had discovered America, da Gama had doubled the Cape, and printed book was superseding medieval manuscript. In England, Henry VII had established the powerful Tudor dynasty, and put an end to baronial wars; and Caxton had printed nearly a hundred separate works.

The Tudor century, however, was one of transition from old to new. Politically, from feudalism to nationalism; in religion, from Catholicism to Protestantism; in the arts, from medieval to classical; in language, from medieval to modern spelling and pronunciation. In 1500 England was merely on the fringe of European culture, and the new age of the Renaissance dawned only slowly. Perhaps the transition is best symbolized in its architecture, when buildings essentially medieval were gradually modified by the addition of classical detail, before the first truly classical buildings were erected early in the following century. And the progress of the language may be summarized in two quotations: the first from Caxton's Prologue to his translation of a French version of the *Aeneid* (*Eneydos*) of 1490:

And that comyn englysshe that is spoken in one shyre varyeth from a nother in so moche that in my dayes happened that certayn marchauntes were in a shippe in tamyse for to haue sayled ouer the see into zelande, and for lacke of wynde thei taryed atte forlond, and wente to lande for to refreshe them.

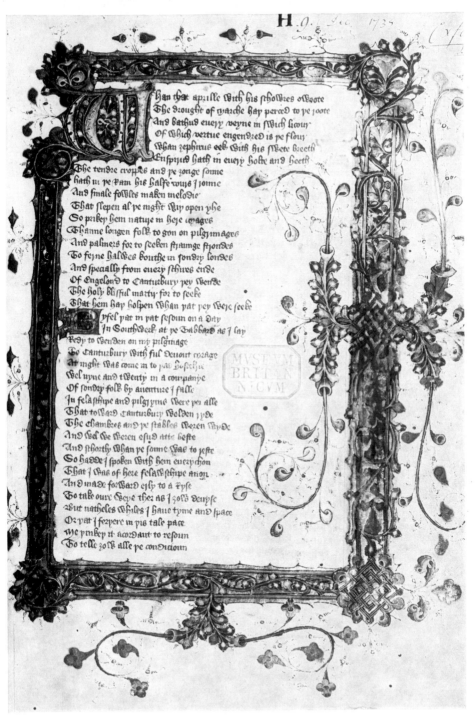

Middle English. Chaucer's *Prologue* to *The Canterbury Tales*, from a manuscript of about 1400.

Whan that Aprill With his shouris sote
And the droughte of marche hath perced y rote
And bapdid euery veyne in suche licour
Of Whiche vertu engendrid is the flour
Whanne zepherus eke With his sote breth
Enspirid hath in euery holte and heth
The tendir croppis and the yong sonne
Hath in the ram half his cours y ronne
And smale foulis make melodie
That sleppyn al nyght With oppyn ye
So prikith hem nature in her corage
Than longyng folk to goon on pilgremage
And palmers to seche straunge londis
To serue haloWis couth in sondry londis
And specially fro euery shiris ende
Of yngelond to Cauntirbury thay Wende
The holy blissful martir for to seke
That them hath holpyn Whan they Were seke
And fil in that seson on a day
In SuthWerk atte tabard as I lay
Redy to Wende on my pilgremage
To Cauntirbury With deuout corage
That nyght Was come in to that hosterye
Wel nyne & tWenty in a companye
Of sondry folk be auenture y falle
In feleship as pilgrympis Were they alle
That toWard Cauntirbury Wolden ryde
The chambris and the stablis Were Wyde
And Wel Were they esid atte beste

Chaucer's *Prologue* as printed by Caxton in 1477. Printing helped to unify dialects and make that of the East Midlands and London, of Caxton and Chaucer, the standard English language.

And one of theym named sheffelde a mercer cam in to an hows and axed for mete, and specyally he axyd after eggys. And the good wyf answerde that she coude speke no frenshe. And the marchaunt was angry for he also coude speke no frenshe, but wold haue hadde egges, and she vnderstode hym not. And thenne at laste a nother sayd that he wolde haue eyren, then the good wyf sayd that she vnderstod hym wel. Loo what sholde a man in thyse dayes now wryte, egges or eyren. Certaynly it is harde to playse euery man by cause of dyuersite and chaunge of langage.

The London ale-wife, for whom eyren were good old English eyren, could not understand the Sheffield mercer with his outlandish Scandinavian eggs (see p. 61).

Then, Thomas Nashe in his *Pierce Penilesse* of 1592:

Our Players are not as the players beyond Sea, a sort of squirting baudie Comedians, that have whores and common Curtizens to playe womens partes, and forbeare no immodest speech or unchast action that may procure laughter; but our Sceane is more statelye furnisht than ever it was in the time of Roscius, our representations honourable, and full of gallant resolution.

In the Epilogue to one of his first printed books Caxton had written, marvelling: "It is not wreton with penne and ynke as other bokes ben . . . for all the bookes of this storye . . . thus enpryntid as ye here see were begonne in oon day, and also fynysshid in oon day". The new invention helped to spread the new ideas and learning of the Renaissance, and encouraged literacy, for books were soon within the reach of most people, at least in towns, and to be able to read was as profitable as it was delightful.

Inevitably, printing had a powerful influence on the English language. For one thing, men of the north and men of the south became acquainted with the East Midland dialect of London, which thus became standard English. Then, printing tended to standardize grammar, usage and spelling. Grammar, however, had been so simplified that there was little room for further simplification, and changes were mainly ones of detail.

For example, Caxton used the Midland form *they ben*, but Nashe wrote *they are*, and in the course of the sixteenth century the final *-n* or *-en* was dropped in verbal plurals, Chaucer's they slepen becoming Shakespeare's they sleep. Similarly, the southern *-eth* of the third person singular became the *-s* of the northern dialect, though even at the end of the century Shakespeare still used both forms: "It blesseth him that gives". Here he wrote *that* where we should write *who*, the relative pronoun that was only then coming into use; and he always used *his* or *it* for the neuter possessive: "It had it head bit off by it young". Only in the seventeenth century did *its* become the established form.

Caxton's spelling was an attempt to reproduce the pronunciation of the English of his age, not an easy task, for the Roman alphabet had never fitted the Teutonic language like a glove. Then, for centuries English had been written and confused by Frenchmen, while English scribes had spelled according to their fancy. Middle English *dette*, taken from Old French, was given a *b* (*debt*) to show its Latin origin (*debitum*), although the *b* was not pronounced; and to Old French *delit* a *gh* was added (*delight*) to bring it into line with *light* (Old English *leoht*, German *Licht*), as a silent *g* was to be slipped into *foreign* (Old French *forain*, Latin *foranus*) because there was a *g* in *reign* (OF. *regne*, L. *regnum*), and an *h* into Celtic-Latin *Tamesa* (Thames) to twin the river with Hebrew *Thomas*.

To add to the confusion, pronunciation had changed and was changing. Perhaps to distinguish themselves from the uncouth provincials of the north and west, fifteenth-century Londoners began to speak more delicately, with closer lips and higher tongue, working their jaws less vigorously, so that the more open vowels became closer, rising, as it were, in the scale from open to close. Chaucer spoke with what we should call a broad accent, not unlike the northerner today, and the difference between the old and new pronunciation resembles that between broad Yorkshire and our present southern speech. The northerner says *man* with fully opened jaw, but the southerner's pronunciation is halfway to *men*. The northerner's *come up* has the broad *u* of *full*, and his *road* is a *rawd*: "T'man's coom oop t'rawd". Chaucer would have understood.

However, short vowels, like consonants, were fairly stable,

the change being mainly, though not entirely, a shift of the long vowels, and a glance at the diagram on page 26 will show what happened. As *ă* tended to rise to *ĕ*, so did *ĕ* to *ā*, *ā* to *ee*, and *ee*, unable to go higher, became a compound of bottom and top, the diphthong *a-ee*, that is, long *i*. Thus *whan* rose to *when*, *agen* to *again*, *swate* to *sweet*, and *feen* changed to *fine* (*fa-een*). Similarly with the back vowels: *rawd—road, fode—food*, and the *oo* of *toun* became the diphthong *ah-oo* of *town*. This is known as the Great Vowel Shift, but as all words with the same vowel were not affected in the same way we have anomalies such as *broad road* and *good food*, which help to account for the vagaries of modern spelling and pronunciation.

By the end of the sixteenth century, when Shakespeare was writing, pronunciation was not unlike that of today, though spelling reflected, as it still does, the speech of the Middle Ages. *Heather* and *broad* are more or less medieval pronunciations, but not *heath* and *road*; the *gh* of words like *night* (ni-ch-t) was no longer pronounced, and already unstressed *a, e, o, u*, once distinctly pronounced, were being reduced to a similar neutral sound, as in "a troublesome undercurrent", where all eight vowels are approximately the same.

Owing to the Norse and Norman invasions, the English had grown used to borrowing from other tongues, and all through the Tudor century of transition new words were pouring into the language. Most of them were Latin, either direct borrowings, or indirect through French, and in this new world of discovery, revival of learning and translation of the classics, many of them were deliberately introduced by scholars to fill gaps in the native vocabulary: *vocabulary* itself, *education, exploration; definite, idolatrous, vertical; eradicate, penetrate, postulate*. A few French adaptations of Latin adaptations of Greek words had already been borrowed in the Middle English period, *philosophy* and *theology*, for example, and now that Greek was being taught at the universities, while men like Erasmus, Dean Colet and Sir Thomas More were promoting its study, and Tyndale translating the New Testament into English, others were inevitably introduced. Again most of these came by way of Latin, like *cylinder, democracy, geography*, but others, such as *catastrophe*, were taken directly from the Greek, and many more were to follow in the next century.

In the Middle Ages it was French and Latin that had so enriched and transformed the native vocabulary, but in the sixteenth century the exploration of the world beyond Europe opened up new, exciting sources of supply. The Spaniards were in the West Indies, the Portuguese in the East, and in addition to the exotic products they brought back with them, came strange words that found their way into English: *alligator, banana, cannibal* (really *caribal,* a West Indian native), *canoe, chocolate* (Mexican *chocolatl*), *hammock, hurricane, potato* (Haitian *batata*), *tomato* (Mexican *tomatl*), *tobacco.*

Then, after the learned disputations and persecutions of the Reformation in the first half of the century, the Elizabethans began to travel in Europe: through France to Italy, to see the art of the Renaissance and treasures of ancient Rome. There they picked up such words as *cupola* (there were no domes in England), *fresco, piazza, sonnet, stanza,* and brought them back to England along with Italian fashions.

This introduction of new words, some pedantic, others affected, by "preachers and schoolmasters, merchants and travellers", was opposed by some purists, notably Thomas Wilson who, in his *Arte of Rhetorike* of 1553, protested against the obscurity of "darke wordes" and "ynkhorne termes", and the affectation of "outlandishe English": "He that cometh lately out of France, will talk Frenche Englishe and never blush at the matter. Another choppes in with English Italianated, and applieth the Italian phrase to our English speaking." And 40 years later, in *Love's Labour's Lost,* Shakespeare good-naturedly made fun of parson Nathaniel's rhetoric: "intituled, nominated, or called"; of the inkhorn terms of schoolmaster Holofernes: "thrasonicall . . . peregrinate . . . abhominable, which he would call abominable"; and of Don Armado's Spanishified English: "the posteriors of this day, which the rude multitude call the after-noone"; "dallie with my excrement, with my mustachio". *Stanza* was always good for a laugh, as when Holofernes says, "Let me heare a staffe, a stanze, a verse", and Jaques in *As You Like It*: "Come, more, another stanzo: Cal you 'em stanzo's?"

Roger Ascham, classical scholar and tutor of the future Queen Elizabeth, thought his native English such a barbarous medley that he wrote it under protest, and More wrote his

Utopia in Latin. But Philip Sidney proudly confessed his own barbarousness, and maintained that English was equal to any tongue in the world "for the uttering sweetly and properly the conceit of the mind, which is the end of speeche". He was only 32 when he died from a wound in 1586 at the beginning of the war with Spain. Had he lived a few years longer, he would have been able to quote Shakespeare to prove his contention.

Shakespeare was fortunate in his age, for when he began to write, about 1590, the English language, freed from its encumbering inflexions, was almost a plastic medium. There were no rules for writing, and no treatises on grammar, for there was no grammar, or virtually none. Almost any word could be used as any part of speech; a noun could serve as a verb: "He childed as I fathered"; so could an adjective: "Time will unfair"; and an adverb: "They askance their eyes"; an adverb could be a noun: "in the dark backward"; and so could an adjective, old for age: "and make my old excuse". A pronoun could be a noun: "the proudest he", "the cruellest she"; or a verb: "if thou thou'st him".

Then, Shakespeare had at his command a wealth, a variety of words such as no other language had ever possessed: Teutonic, Scandinavian, French, Latin, with a scattering of Greek and newly imported words from the Romance tongues. In *Hamlet* the short English *u* sound gives an ominous undertone to the tragedy: *mother, suffer, hugger-mugger, trouble a woman*; in *Macbeth* the Scandinavian gutturals create an atmosphere of cruelty and confinement: *shake, take, thick, scarf, rooky*; and in the later plays polysyllabic latinisms abound, often contrasted with simple English monosyllables: "monumental alabaster", "multitudinous seas incarnadine", "To lie in cold obstruction and to rot".

Shakespeare sometimes laughed at himself for using these neologisms, as when he makes Shallow say: "Better accommodated? it is good, yea indeede is it: good phrases are surely, and ever were very commendable. Accommodated, it comes of *Accommodo*: very good, a good Phrase." *Commendable* was a Middle English borrowing, but Shakespeare seems to have been the first to use *accommodate* in this sense, to furnish with: "A Souldier is better accommodated than with a Wife". And he introduced scores of other new words and usages: *conflux, control* (noun), *credent, dwindle, homekeeping, illume, incarnadine* (verb), *lonely, monumental, multitudinous, orb* (globe), *plausive* . . .

Yet, in spite of all these foreign adoptions, the language remained, as it still remains, essentially English. All the humble but indispensable working-parts of speech are English: prepositions (*by, with, from, to, of*), conjunctions (*and, but*), and auxiliaries (*be, have, do, shall, must*). And nearly all our fundamental nouns and verbs are English: *birth, life, mother, father, man, woman, blood, child, bone, heart, world, earth, house, hearth, fire, food, plough, spade, dig, wheat, bread, milk, rain, water, light, sun, clothes, word, eat, drink, speak, write, laugh, weep, mourn, walk, run, dream, sleep, die. Air*, it is true, is French-Latin, but most words so derived are refinements rather than fundamentals, and English remains basically the language of the Anglo-Saxon invaders of Britain, though wonderfully diversified with words of foreign extraction.

10

MODERN ENGLISH

In 1599 Shakespeare's contemporary, Samuel Daniel, wrote prophetically:

> And who in time knowes whither we may vent
> The treasure of our tongue, to what strange shores
> This gaine of our best glorie shal be sent,
> T'inrich vnknowing Nations with our stores?
> What worlds in th'yet vnformed occident
> Shall come refin'd with th'accents that are ours?

It was to be only a few years before the English tongue was carried to the shores of Virginia, where the first English settlement was made at Jamestown in 1607; and then in 1620 the Pilgrim Fathers landed at Plymouth, Massachusetts. With them these Puritan emigrants, fleeing from religious persecution, took the recently published Authorized Version of the Bible, a treasure of our tongue indeed. This was based on earlier translations, and on the whole its language was old-fashioned, with comparatively few latinisms, yet the beauty of many of its finest passages depends on the interplay of Old English words with those of Latin derivation: "How doth the *city* sit *solitary*, that was full of *people*! how is she become as a widow! she that was great among the *nations*, and *princess* among the *provinces*, how is she become *tributary*!" Seven of these thirty-five words, one in five—*city, solitary, people, nations, princess, provinces, tributary* —are Latin, taken from Old French during the Middle Ages.

The complex music of this apparently simple passage of prose can best be appreciated by printing it clause by clause and phrase by phrase, from the icy isolating sibilants and short *i*'s of the first line to the variation on the refrain, in which Old English "as a widow" is transformed into Latin *tributary*,

87

so linking end with beginning by a near-rhyme with another four-syllabled Latin word, *solitary*. There is much more than this, of course, but it should be noted that all the words of Latin origin have from two to four syllables, and all but one are prominently at the end of a line, contrasting with the two English disyllables, *become* and *widow*:

> How doth the *city* sit *solitary*,
> that was full of *people*!
> how is she become
> as a widow!
> she that was great
> among the *nations*,
> and *princess*
> among the *provinces*,
> how is she become
> *tributary*!

The number of French, and therefore Latin, words entering the language had reached its climax in the age of Chaucer (1350–1400), and by the middle of the seventeenth century had dropped considerably, so many having already been incorporated, yet writers of the period delighted in the exploitation of sonorous Latin polysyllables: Milton, for example:

> Anon, out of the earth, a *fabric huge*
> Rose like an *exhalation*, with the *sound*
> Of *dulcet symphonies* and *voices* sweet,
> Built like a *temple*, where *pilasters* round
> Were set, and *Dorick pillars* overlaid
> With golden *architrave*; nor did there want
> *Cornice* or *frieze*, with *bossy sculptures* graven.

These lines from *Paradise Lost*, in which the proportion of Latin to English words is one to three, illustrate a more scholarly interest in classical art than that of the Italianate Elizabethan. The first truly classical buildings were going up in England, and *Doric*, of course, is Greek, but, although their immediate source was French, *pilaster*, *architrave*, *cornice* come from Italian. *Symphony* was a Middle English borrowing, but a number of musical terms now began to be taken direct from Italian, many of them brought by Royalists who, like John Evelyn, travelled abroad during the Commonwealth period: *madrigal, fugue, opera, solo, sonata, oboe*; and there were new words descriptive of the visual arts: *gesso, dado, bas-relief, chiaroscuro*. In this way, further variety and the music of final vowels was added to the language.

The seventeenth century was the great age of Dutch painting, the age of Rembrandt, and English borrowed from yet another store of words: *easel* (Dutch *ezel*—an ass, bearer of burdens, like a clothes-*horse*), *landscape, etch, sketch*. Dutch, too, are a number of nautical terms that commemorate English respect for their rivals at sea: *avast* (hold fast), *boom* (English *beam*), *cruise, sloop, yacht* (from *jagen*—to hunt). Then there is the strange word *gas*, coined by the chemist Van Helmont from the Greek *chaos*, a void.

With the Restoration in 1660 there was a revival of French influence, for Charles II had spent most of his youth in exile in France. In some ways it was an unfortunate influence, for French culture at this time was hidebound, fettered by pedants to a slavish adherence to classical rules and the cult of Reason. Happily, the English are not given to extremes, and Dryden, Pope, Johnson, the leading figures of the neo-classical age of English literature, interpreted the ancients more liberally than the French. Chaucer, however, they found scarcely comprehensible, and Shakespeare something of a barbarian who had neglected his Aristotle; and Dryden polished the language of the *Canterbury Tales*, and refashioned *The Tempest* and *Antony and Cleopatra* as they should have been written.

By the end of the century, when Dryden died, and his mantle was about to fall upon Pope, it seemed to the cultured minority that England had entered another Augustan Age: an age of smoothness and correctness, of marble in place of brick, like that of the early Roman Empire of Augustus Caesar, Virgil, Horace and Livy. And yet there was a feeling of unease, which we can understand: a fear that they were writing for oblivion, that in another 300 years their language might be as antiquated and unread as that of 300 years before in their own day, a fear expressed by Pope: "Our sons their fathers' failing language see, / And such as Chaucer is, shall Dryden be". The English language was changing as they wrote: new words, cant terms, uncertain usages; yet there was no authority to which they could appeal, no Academy, as there was in France, to standardize usage, no dictionary to define meaning and fix pronunciation, not even a book of grammar to demonstrate the correct way to speak and write.

Yet they need not have worried. Dryden and Pope, Addison and Swift are as readable today as Auden and Shaw; the language has altered little in the last three centuries, apart from inevitable additions to the vocabulary, and some changes of meaning and pronunciation. Thus, *sad* has changed from *serious* to *mournful, stout* from *valiant* to *corpulent*; and in 1700 *fault* rhymed with *fought, take* with *tack, joined* with *mind*.

One development, however, is worth noting. In Shakespeare's time the normal way of expressing the present tense was in the form I write or I do write, but by the time of Pope I am writing had become a regular usage. There is an obvious advantage in being able to distinguish between the true present and the present of habit, between I am writing (now) and I write (sometimes), and English is the only language that can do so thus easily. The analogous passive form, The book is being written, was developed in the eighteenth century. Except in dialect—I do belong (ought) to write—the use of *do* as an auxiliary has become restricted to the negative and interrogative: I don't write, Did you write? and the emphatic I *do* write! This use of *do* and *did*, although making for clarity, is puzzling to learners of the language.

It is not quite true to say that there was no English dictionary in 1700. A number of compilations had appeared in the seventeenth century, but these were selective, confined to more difficult words, and it was not until 1721 that Nathaniel Bailey published what he called "A more compleat universal etymological English dictionary than any extant". This was an important advance, and formed a basis for Dr Johnson's famous work. Johnson summarized the position in the middle of the eighteenth century:

When I took the first survey of my undertaking, I found our speech copious without order, and energetick without rules: wherever I turned my view, there was perplexity to be disentangled, and confusion to be regulated; choice was to be made out of boundless variety, without any established principle of selection; adulterations were to be detected, without a settled test of purity; and modes of expression to be rejected or received, without the suffrages of any writers of classical reputation or acknowledged authority.

In 1755, after seven years as "a harmless drudge"—Johnson's own definition of lexicographer—his *Dictionary of the English Language* was published in two volumes, containing more than 2,000 pages of definitions, from the simplest to the most erudite words. Sometimes these were not very helpful—"Pox: pustules; efflorencies; exanthematous eruptions"—but generally they were clear and simple. Etymology was often shaky, for Johnson was no scholar of Old or Middle English, but pronunciation was aided by indicating stressed syllables, usage illustrated by numerous quotations from acknowledged authorities, and with few exceptions—*energetick*, for example—spelling was that of today.

Shakespeare had no dictionary to consult, and today it is difficult to imagine being unable to refer to any authority for the meaning, derivation, spelling, pronunciation and use of a word; and correspondingly easy to understand why Johnson's *Dictionary* was hailed as such an extraordinary achievement. In that static Augustan Age there were those who wished to "fix" the language, but Johnson had come to see the impossibility as well as folly of trying to "embalm" it, though he did more than any other man to give "longevity to that which its own nature forbids to be immortal". For that reason, perhaps, he "would never consent to disgrace the walls of Westminster Abbey with an English inscription". Goldsmith's epitaph had to be in Latin: a language long dead, embalmed, unchanging, immortal as language can be.*

The grammarians followed, and settled or suggested, with more or less pedantry, the proper way to speak and write English—the correct use of shall and will; averse from, not to; different from but indifferent to—and by 1800 the syntax of

* Even as recently as 1905 Thomas Hardy composed a Latin inscription for a memorial, in the belief that "the English language was liable to undergo great changes in the future".

Wordsworth, Coleridge and Jane Austen was little different from that of today. But the neo-classical age was over, and with it the inflated, latinized diction of its verse; there was a return to the Middle Ages for inspiration, and Wordsworth began to write in "a selection of language really used by men":

> It is the first mild day of March,
> Each minute sweeter than before:
> The redbreast sings from the tall larch
> That stands beside our door.

It was not a return to Middle English, but the verse has the fresh simplicity of a medieval ballad, and there are only two words—*March, minute*—of Latin origin.

Britain lost her first Empire in 1776, when the thirteen American colonies broke away to form a republic with a history independent of the mother country, from which it was separated by 3,000 miles of sea. It was more than 150 years since the first settlements had been made, and by this time there were some four million Americans, most of them British in origin, and living along the east coast, from New England to Georgia. Already there were differences between the language spoken in England and in America. The English had begun to ignore the *r* at the end of a word and before a consonant, so that *letter* was pronounced *letta*, and *fort* became indistinguishable from *fought*; and in southern English the broad *a* of *father* was replacing the flat *a* of *man* in words like *bath* and *castle*. The Americans, however, spoke more deliberately and conscientiously, and generally preserved the older pronunciation, as they also preserved a number of words and expressions that had dropped out of use in England: the old past participle *gotten*, for example, and the Chaucerian I guess for I should think: "Of twenty yeer of age he was, I gesse". Then, there were inevitable additions to the vocabulary, words, many of them American-Indian, descriptive of life in a vast new world unknown to the English: *moccasin, moose, skunk, tomahawk*, and the early nineteenth-century *toboggan*.

As the Americans, joined by emigrants from other parts of Europe, opened up their semi-continent, pressing ever west and south, they developed a nationalist spirit that rejected the speech of England as their standard, and began to think of their language as American rather than English. One of the leaders of this movement was Noah Webster, who in 1789 wrote "An Essay on the Necessity . . . of Reforming the Mode of Spelling": "Now is the time, and *this* the country, in which we may expect success, in attempting changes favorable to language, science and government. . . . Let us then seize the present moment, and establish a *national language*, as well as a national government." And in 1828 he published his *American Dictionary of the English Language*. Here were words unknown to Johnson, and spellings of which he would have disapproved; yet *defense, labor* (Latin *defensum, labor*) are more defensible than *defence, labour,* and the first London playhouse was the Theater, though *theatre, centre* (L. *theatrum, centrum*) seem to be the better spellings. Again, *program,* before being brought into line with French *programme,* was the English spelling taken by the early colonists to America, and *telegram,* "a new Yankee word" in 1857, naturally followed. And *catalog* (L. *catalogus* from Greek *katalogos*) is as good as *catalogue.* The English have adopted *medieval* instead of *mediæval,* but instead of the American *jail* generally retain the perplexing *gaol,* of which Johnson wrote: "It is always pronounced and too often written *jail*" (see p. 76).

Meanwhile a second British Empire had come into being, and with it came a host of strange new words, such as *bangle, bungalow* (Bengal), *chintz, cot, dinghy, loot, veranda* from India; *gong, amuck* from Malaya; *taboo* and *tattoo* (the skin) from Polynesia; *boomerang* and *kangaroo* from Australia. *Tea* is Chinese, *coffee* and *horde* are Turkish, and *pyjamas* Persian. *Hurricane,* used by Shakespeare, had come from the West Indies, *typhoon* from China, and in the early nineteenth century came the splendid coinage, *blizzard,* from America.

Until the end of the eighteenth century the sources of power had been wind, water and the horse; machines were made of wood, and artificial light was that of the candle. But the nineteenth century was the age of the Industrial Revolution, of steam-power, steel and the factory system, and of gas for lighting. New words were needed for all the new sciences, discoveries and inventions, many of them coined from Greek: *photo-graph* (light-writing), *tele-phone* (far-sound). The Germans, who prefer to make compounds of native words, as did their

93

Anglo-Saxon cousins, have *Fernsprecher*, as for *hydrogen* (water-producing) they have *Wasserstoff*, and for *biology* (life-lore) *Lebenslehre*.

In the twentieth century the pace of scientific progress has doubled and redoubled. It began with electricity, motor car, aeroplane and cinema (Greek *kinema*, movement, movies), and we enter its final decades with a knowledge of nuclear fission and the ability to send "live" photographs from the moon. The new words that, as a result, have entered the language, would fill a volume: from *automobile, garage, petrol*, taken from French; *camouflage* and *blitz*, products of two world wars; to *allergy, astronaut* (star sailor), *computer, helicopter* (screw-wing), *laser, proton, television*. On the other hand, many of the words that we associate with our own age have remarkably long histories: *refrigerator* (1611), *technology* (1615), *electricity* (1646, from Greek *elektron*, amber), *aeronautics* (1753). The dates are those of the first known use of the words as given in the *Oxford English Dictionary*, but there may be others still earlier. Of course their seventeenth- to eighteenth-century meanings were very different from ours. Of electricity, for example, Johnson wrote:

A property in some bodies, whereby, when rubbed, so as to grow warm, they draw little bits of paper, or such like substances, to them.

Such was the account given a few years ago of electricity; but . . . The philosophers are now endeavouring to intercept the strokes of lightning.

In fact, Benjamin Franklin had just done so—in 1752.

Language itself has been reduced to a science, *linguistics*, with its own terminology. *Phonetics*: the science of sounds in speech, and their representation by symbols. The letters of the Roman alphabet cannot represent all the sounds, particularly vowels, in English—*pall, pale, pal, pare, part*—and symbols are needed for all such variations on the vowel *a*. *Semantics*: the science of meaning in language. *Phoneme*: a unit of sound that changes meaning: *a*-ll, *i*-ll; *bl*-ush, *cr*-ush. *Morpheme*: a grammatical unit that changes meaning: *re-creat-ion, creat-or-s*.

Slang, highly colloquial language that is not accepted as standard, there must always have been. The Romans had it:

testa (pot), for example, was vulgar Latin for *caput* (head), and from it was derived the French *tête*; and Eric Partridge, the authority on slang, derives the word itself from *sling*, "language slung about", as in the phrase of *c.* 1400: "The bolde wordes that [he] did sling". Dr Johnson called it *cant*: "a corrupt dialect used by beggars and vagabonds ... barbarous jargon", and he dismissed *woundy* as "a low bad word", and *banter* as "barbarous, without etymology". *Woundy* (excessive) has disappeared, but *banter* has survived, as have many other words that were originally slang: *bus* (omnibus, for all), *hoax, jamboree, joke, kidnap* (nab kids), *patter* (paternoster?), *sham* ("a low word"), *shambling* ("a low bad word"), *van* (from Persian *caravan*), and vivid metaphors such as *above-board, below the belt.*

Much of our modern slang comes from America, some of it from the Black Americans, descendants of former African slaves. As *banana* and *yam* are Wolof words, a language of the Guinea coast from which many African slaves were taken, the Wolof tongue may well be the source of *dig* (*dega*, understand), *hippy* (*hipi*, become aware), *OK* (*waw kay*, all right).*

Most slang is ephemeral, the colloquial speech of a decade, but if it has any permanent value it will be accepted into the language, and some current slang—*beatnik, bouncer* (chucker out)—has already been included, though not necessarily with approval, in the *Oxford English Dictionary.*

This great work, originally called *A New English Dictionary on Historical Principles*, was begun as long ago as 1857, but it was 1884 before the first part was published, and 1928 before it was completed. Such a work can never be complete, however, and a supplementary volume was added in 1933, and the first of three new volumes that will supersede it appeared in 1972. No other language has such a dictionary, for not only does it attempt to list every known word in English since the year 1000, but it also gives the history of each, illustrated by quotations showing its use since its first known appearance, ranging from *Beowulf* to the present day. It is a far cry from the Old English of,

> Þæt wæs þam gomelan gingæste word
> breostgehygdum, ær he bæl cure,

* See the article by David Dalby in *The Times*, 19 July 1969.

hate heaðowylmas: him of hreðre gewat
sawol secean soðfæstra dom,

to the Preface to the *Oxford Dictionary*, written by its chief editor, James Murray: "That vast aggregate of words and phrases which constitutes the Vocabulary of English-speaking men presents, to the mind that endeavours to grasp it as a definite whole, the aspect of one of those nebulous masses familiar to the astronomer, in which a clear and unmistakable nucleus shades off on all sides." *Beowulf* was composed in the synthetic language of the Anglo-Saxon invaders of Britain, with its elaborate system of genders and inflexions, and completely Teutonic vocabulary. Murray's prose is analytic, and its vocabulary epitomizes more than 1,000 years of history: Christian conversion, Norse invasion, Norman Conquest, adoption of French words in the Middle Ages, then, so accustomed to borrowing had the language become, of Latin and Greek at the Renaissance, and finally of words from all quarters of the globe. Below is a summary, taken from the *Oxford Dictionary*, of the foreign words in this passage:

Vast, 1575, from Latin *vastus*, void, immense.

Aggregate, Middle English, f. L. *aggregatus*. An assemblage of units, 1650.

Phrase, 1530, f. Late Latin *phrasis*, f. Greek *phrazo*, tell.

Constitute, 1477, f. L. *constituere*, to set up. To make a thing what it is, 1848.

Vocabulary, 1532, medieval Latin *vocabularius*, a list of words. The sum of the words composing a language, 1782.

Present (verb), ME. f. Old French *presenter*. To exhibit, 1500.

Endeavour, ME. f. F. *en-devoir*, make it one's duty.

Definite, 1530, f. L. *definitus*, distinct, precise.

Aspect, ME. f. L. *aspectus*. Appearance presented to the eye, 1594; to the mind, 1704.

Nebulous, late ME. f. L. *nebulosus*, cloudy. Applied to stars, 1679.

Mass, late ME. f. OF. *masse*, f. L. *massa*, f. Greek *maza*, barley-cake, dough.

Familiar, ME. f. OF. *familier*, f. L. *familia*, household.

Astronomer, ME. f. OF., f. L., f. Gk. *astronomos*, star-arranging.

Kirby Hall, Northants, built when Shakespeare was a boy. The visual equivalent of what happened to the English language: French and classical elaborations added to a native fabric.

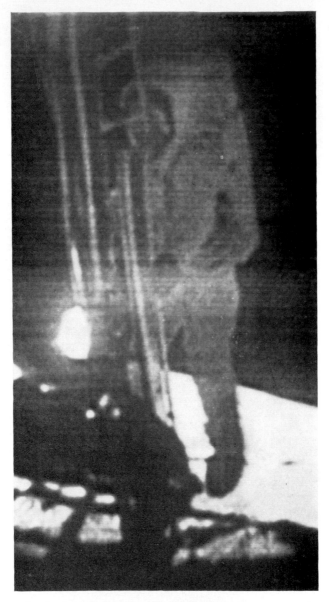

And who in time knowes whither we may vent
The treasure of our tongue?

Samuel Daniel, *Musophilus*, 1599

21 July 1969. The American astronaut, Neil
Armstrong, about to step on to the moon.

Clear, ME. & OF. *cler,* L. *clarus.*
Mistake (verb), ME. f. Old Norse *mistaka*; (noun) 1638;
    unmistakable, 1666.
Nucleus, 1704, L. *nucleus,* kernel, f. *nux,* nut.

The nucleus of this nebulous mass is composed of Old English words, from which radiates a galaxy of other words, dialectical, slang, technical, scientific, foreign, more and more remotely English, until they fade imperceptibly into the surrounding darkness. "The circle of the English language has a well-defined centre but no discernible circumference."

THE EXCELLENCY OF THE
ENGLISH TONGUE

WHEN RICHARD CAREW wrote his essay on "The Excellencie of the English Tongue" at the beginning of the seventeenth century, Shakespeare was writing his greatest plays, in a language that differed little from our own. Spelling, however, was still unsettled; on the same day he signed himself both *Shakspere* and *Shakspeare*, and if the addition to the manuscript play of *Sir Thomas More* is in his hand, he wrote *voyce*, *comaund*, *stilnes*, *hows*, *plaigue*, *lyvd*, *wer*, *woold*, *tane* (taken), *gott*. Although spelling was virtually standardized by the end of the century, it represented, more or less, the pronunciation of Chaucer rather than of Dryden, and even less that of today. Before considering the excellencies of the English tongue, therefore, it may be as well to consider its defects.

Much the most important of these, whether we call it defect or mere difficulty, is its spelling. If *meat* rhymes with *meet*, how should we pronounce *great*, *create*, *bread*, *heart*? Why does not *have* rhyme with *save*? *door* (as in northern dialect) with *poor*? How explain the pronunciation of *chair*, *choir*, *coil*? *hanging* and *changing*? *bough*, *bought*, *cough*, *dough*, *rough*, and *four hours*? *over*, *cover*, *hover*, *mover*? *are*, *pare*, *pair*, *pear*, *fear*? And consider the sequence *won*, *one*, *gone*, *lone*, *loan*, *blown*, *clown*, *sound*, *wound*, *swoon*, *rune*, *tune*, *hewn*, *sewn*. . . . There are more than 60 ways of spelling our long vowels, and even some of the short vowels are unreliable: *cut*, *put*; *busy*, *bury*; *let*, *ate*; *gather*, *father*. Consonants, too, can be equally disconcerting. Sometimes they are ignored (or ignawd): *scent* (scant), *reign* (rein, rain), *doubt* (out), *talk* (talc), *overturn*, *climb*, *knife*, *thought*, *yacht*. Sometimes *t* becomes *sh*: *note—notion*; and *s* changes to *zh*: *fuss—fusion*, or to *z*: *dose—rose*; and we say *books*, *cats*, *steps*, but *volumez*, *dogz*, *stairz*. This last eccentricity is logical—up to a point. An unvoiced consonant is followed by the unvoiced *s*, a voiced consonant by the voiced *z*. It is easier to say books than bookz, dogz than dogs—yet stairz might well rhyme with scarce, piecez with thesis.

The Roman alphabet could not represent all the vowel, or even consonantal, sounds in English, and the system of diphthongs, as in *oil* and *out*, and digraphs, whereby two letters express one sound, like the *ea* and *th* of *death*, broke down with the fifteenth-century vowel shift and other changes of pronunciation, such as the omission of the guttural *gh* in words like *night*. Rules may be given: *ch* is pronounced as in *arch*, but what about *architect*? and *chord*? *sc* before *e* and *i* is pronounced *s*, as in *scene*, *science*, but what about *sceptic*? sensibly spelled *skeptic* by the Americans.

English spelling is a matter of exceptions rather than of rules, and although picturesque, it must be admitted that it is as illogical as so many other things English (our public schools, for example, are private), and there are those who, like Bernard Shaw, would reform it altogether. A few simplifications could easily be made: *hav* for *have*, *hillz* for *hills*, *dhe* for *the*, *det* for *debt*, but there are difficulties about extensive alteration. For example, if *ai* were the accepted symbol for long *a*, *rain*, *rein*, *reign* would be identical when written, as would other homophones: *would*, *wood*; *there*, *their*; *sea*, *see*; *sun*, *son*; *hire*, *higher*. Then, if we were to write *naishun*, the Frenchman (who also does not pronounce as he spells) would not recognize his native *nation*, or many of the other countless words derived from French. We should be making the written language more difficult to understand for many foreigners: Italians, Spaniards and Portuguese as well as French.

Again, what pronunciation is spelling to represent? There are two main standards: English and American. The American is generally more conscientious about pronouncing all his syllables, and whereas the English say *nécess'ry*, he says *necessairy*. His *can't* rhymes with *cant* (quite logically), and the *a* of words like *bath* and *dance* is as flat as that of *hath* and *stance*. Yet his short *o* of *not*, *top*, *rod* is more like *naht*, *tahp*, *rahd*. H. L. Mencken, author of *The American Language*, was in no doubt as to which is the better:

The American of today is much more honestly English, in any sense that Shakespeare would have understood, than the so-called Standard English of England. It still shows all the characters that marked the common tongue in the days of Elizabeth, and it continues to resist stoutly the policing that ironed out Standard English in the Seventeenth and Eighteenth Centuries. Standard English must always strike an American as a bit stilted and precious. Its vocabulary is patently less abundant than his own, it has lost to an appreciable extent its old capacity for bold metaphor, and in pronunciation and spelling it seems to him to be extremely uncomfortable and not a little ridiculous. When he hears a speech in its Oxford (or Public-School) form he must be a Bostonian to avoid open mirth. He believes, and on very plausible grounds, that American is better on all counts— clearer, more rational, and above all, more charming.

More rational—yes. But more charming? To the Englishman, Standard American, "spoken almost uniformly by 125 million people", is flat, toneless and mono'nous—for so many of them forget their *t's*—Wa'erga'e, for example.

There is another argument against a radical alteration of English spelling. Most of our words are natural growths, and to change their appearance is like substituting an artificial for a living flower. A word is history in little, revealing its origin, Teutonic perhaps, or Latin, and the way in which it has developed throughout the adventurous centuries, much as some old church, founded in Saxon times, added to and restored from Norman Conquest to Reformation, is a chronicle of wasted time. The phrase is Shakespeare's, *wasted* meaning expended, past, but print it "kronnikul uv waistid teim" and the magic, too, is wasted. Poetry, of course, is primarily aural, its sound, but there is also a visual beauty of association in its written image.

Apart from spelling, nouns present little difficulty, so blessedly free from inflexions are they, except the final *'s, s', s* of genitive and plural. It is true that *children* and *oxen* retain the old Wessex plural in -*en*, and that a few more plurals are irregular: *geese, men, mice, sheep, teeth*; but they are so few that they merely throw into relief the simplicity of the English plural, and it is scarcely worth while changing *children* to *childs*, and *mice* to *mouses*—or should it be *mouzez*, like *houzez*?

Strong verbs are another irregularity, and therefore difficulty. Most of our verbs are weak, forming their past tense and participle by the addition of *-ed*: *I add, added, have added*; but a strong verb changes its root vowel and usually forms its participle with *-en*: *speak, spoke, spoken*; *write, wrote, written*. There are many variations, however: *sing, sang, sung*; *do, did, done*; *get, got, got*, or American—and Old English—*gotten*, as in *forgotten*, though in *I Henry IV*, *c.* 1598, Shakespeare made Hotspur say, "I have forgot the map". Admittedly strong verbs are an "unnecessary" difficulty and have to be learned, but there are not many of them and they are generally easier to pronounce than the weak form: *drove* and *driven* than *drived*, *swam* and *swum* than *swimmed*, and probably for this reason a few old weak verbs have become strong, as *dug* has been preferred to *digged*. In Middle English the *e* of weak endings was always pronounced (Chaucer and Caxton would have said *pronouncéd*), but by the end of the seventeenth century it had become silent except after the dentals *d* and *t*. We cannot say *glid'd* or *wait'd*, but we can and do say, *robb'd, lock'd, kiss'd, breath'd, mov'd* and so on. This English passion for abbreviation led Addison to protest in 1711:

> The same natural Aversion to Loquacity has of late Years made a very considerable Alteration in our Language, by closing in one Syllable the Termination of our Præter-perfect Tense, as in the Words *drown'd, walk'd, arriv'd*, for *drowned, walked, arrived*, which has very much disfigured the Tongue, and turn'd a tenth part of our smoothest Words into so many Clusters of Consonants. This is the more remarkable, because the want of Vowels in our Language has been the general Complaint of our politest Authors, who nevertheless are the Men that have made these Retrenchments, and consequently very much increased our former Scarcity.

And in the following year Swift wrote to the Earl of Oxford proposing the institution of an Academy for the improvement of and "*fixing* our language":

What does your Lordship think of the Words *Drudg'd,
Disturb'd, Rebuk't, Fledg'd*, and a thousand others, every where
to be met in Prose as well as Verse? Where, by leaving out a
Vowel to save a Syllable, we form so jarring a Sound, and
so difficult to utter, that I have often wondred how it could
ever obtain. . . .

This perpetual Disposition to shorten our Words, by
retrenching the Vowels, is nothing else but a tendency to
lapse into the Barbarity of those *Northern* Nations from whom
we are descended, and whose Languages labour all under
the same Defect.

Addison and Swift were thinking of prose and ordinary speech,
for poets had long been omitting (or retaining) the *e* of *-ed*
when it was metrically helpful to do so. Thus, in *The Progress
of the Soul*, 1601, Donne had written:

> A swan . . .
> Glided along, and as he glided watch'd,
> And with his arched necke this poore fish catch'd.
> It mov'd with state, as if to looke upon
> Low things it scorn'd, and yet before that one
> Could thinke he sought it, he had swallow'd cleare
> This, and much such, and unblam'd devour'd there
>   All, but who too swift, too great, or well armed were. *

And after the Battle of Blenheim in 1704 Addison himself
wrote:

> The fatal day its mighty course began,
> That the griev'd world had long desir'd in vain:
> States that their new captivity bemoan'd,
> Armies of martyrs that in exile groan'd,
> Sighs from the depth of gloomy dungeons heard,
> And prayers in bitterness of soul prefer'd,
> *Europe's* loud cries, that Providence assail'd,
> And ANNA's ardent vows, at length prevail'd.

* Note the rhymes: *watch* as *match*; *clear* (from Old French *clair*) and *were*
like modern *there*. In northern dialect *were* still rhymes with *there*, *one* (and
none) with *on* (and *gone*).

Nevertheless there was some truth in his and Swift's strictures, though less than half the truth, for abbreviation has been "retrenching the *Consonants*" rather than the vowels. They did not know that, with very few exceptions, Chaucer pronounced all his consonants—*g-naw*, *k-nock*, *w-rong*, *ha-l-f*, *thou-gh-t* (tho-ch-t)—so that development has been away from Teutonic consonants and gutturals. Yet *drudg'd* and *fledg'd* are admittedly uncouth with their five consonants to one sharp vowel (though a reserve of uncouth words is invaluable when describing the uncouth, and to have such a reserve may be counted an excellency), and how much pleasanter than *mak'd*, *tak'd*, *break'd* are *made*, *took*, *broken*—though *bade*, *book* or *boken* for *bak'd* seem less satisfactory. It would be easy to weaken our remaining strong verbs, to say *I speak'd*, *he fall'd*, *they have think'd*, but the strong form generally sounds better; and then, a little variety in our otherwise simple verbs is preferable to an imposed uniformity. Besides, with only one or two exceptions, all strong verbs are Old English (*strive* is Middle English from French *estriver*) and it would be a pity to obscure their origin.

In an uninflected language like English much use must be made of prepositions, such as *of*, *to*, *by*, *with*, *from*. The Romans could say *homini*, but as we have no inflected dative case we must say *to the man*—although *I gave it the man* is possible and, even less satisfactorily, *I will write the man*. This is easy enough, but *fight with* and *fight against* are less easy: and can we logically disagree as well as agree *with*? Egyptian English is experimental. Not long ago at one entry to Memphis was the legend "Welcome in Memphis", at the other "Welcome at Memphis". Although it may be claimed that *like* is a preposition, and its use as a conjunction grammatically wrong—He ran like I did—most of our prepositional usages are a matter of idiom rather than of grammar (would it be better to omit this second *of*?), and their correct use is a difficulty, an inevitable defect, of (or *in*?) an analytic language. And such a sentence as the newspaper headline: "Rejection *of* pleas *by* rebel unions *against* suspension *for* registering *under* Industrial Act", scarcely makes *for* significancy.

But the defects and difficulties of English are relatively few, and one of the four excellencies that Carew claimed for the English tongue was Easiness.

The first and principal point sought in every language is that we may express the meaning of our minds aptly each to other. Next, that we may do it readily, without great ado. Then fully, so as others may throughly conceive us. And last of all handsomely, that those to whom we speak may take pleasure in hearing us; so as whatsoever tongue will gain the race of perfection must run on these four wheels: *Significancy*, *Easiness*, *Copiousness*, and *Sweetness*, of which the two foremost import a necessity, the two latter a delight.

By Significancy (apparently the first literary use of the word) Carew meant accurate expression of meaning. He found our interjections particularly expressive: *"Phy*! as if therewithal we should spit". *Moldwarp* (mole) "expresses the nature of that beast", as indeed it does, "a thrower up of soil"; and *doomsday* is a sentence in a word. Then, oddly, *grave* means "divers things: sober, a tomb, and to carve"; oddly, because such diversity of meaning makes for ambiguity rather than accuracy of expression, and might be reckoned a defect.

Today we can adduce better instances of significancy. For example, we can express the possessive case by the addition of *-'s* or by using the preposition *of*: earth's fruits or fruits of the earth. German has one form, French the other, but neither has both, nor, therefore, the means of making a subtle distinction of emphasis and meaning. Consider Shakespeare's use of the two forms in Sonnets 12 and 30:

> Then of thy beauty do I question make,
> That thou among the wastes of time must go.

> When to the sessions of sweet silent thought
> I summon up remembrance of things past,
> I sigh the lack of many a thing I sought,
> And with old woes new wail my dear time's waste.

Another cause of significancy in English is its ability to use a noun as an adjective: an oak table, winter migrant, a Chippendale chair, Paddington Station. This attributive, adjectival, use of the noun is different from the compound noun, in which two nouns become one, as in *armchair*, *seaside*.

Oak and *winter* are separate words, half-noun half-adjective, as are *Paddington* and *Chippendale*, and such verbal versatility and compactness are characteristically English.

Easiness. Carew admitted that foreigners found the pronunciation of English difficult, that neither French nor Italian could "utter" such words as *hedge* and *water*. On the other hand, the Englishman, given time, found no difficulty in pronouncing all their words like a native. Which did not prove the inferiority of the English tongue, but merely the superiority of English men; though there is no reason to think that the Elizabethan was a more accomplished linguist than his notoriously incompetent neo-Elizabethan successor.

Carew was on safer ground when he wrote: "neither are we loaden with those declensions, flexions and variations which are incident to many other tongues, but a few articles govern all our verbs and nouns, and so we read a very short grammar". Here he touches briefly, all too briefly, on one of the principal excellencies of the English tongue. We have only one declension of nouns and, with the exception of a dozen irregular plurals, all are treated in the same way, having only the -*s* inflexion of genitive and plural. And adjectives, including *a* and *the*, have no declension, no inflexions at all; we say "the small boy—boy's—boys—boys' ... girl's ... books". Carew might have added that we have no grammatical gender. In French, *sun* is masculine, *moon* feminine; in German, *sun* is feminine, *moon* masculine; in English, both are neuter. Male is masculine *he*, female feminine *she*, a thing neuter *it*.

Again, there is really only one conjugation of verbs (though to be is exceptional*) and, given a knowledge of the past tense and participle forms of strong verbs, anybody who can conjugate one can conjugate them all: I walk (run), he walks (runs), we—you—they walk (run), I—he—we—you—they walked (ran), and so on. The only irregularity is the -*s* of he

* Almost as complex as its German, Latin and French equivalents:

I am	Ich bin	sum	je suis
he is	er ist	est	il est
we are	wir sind	sumus	nous sommes
I was	Ich war	eram	j'étais
you were	ihr wart	eratis	vous étiez
they will be	sie werden sein	erunt	ils seront
they have been	sie sind gewesen	fuerunt	ils ont été

walks (runs), an unnecessary letter that might be dropped. It is important to appreciate the simplicity of English grammar in comparison with the inflexional complexities of Latin, German and Old English.

Having shown that English possesses the two essentials of any language that aspires to excellence, Significancy and Easiness, Carew goes on to consider its delights, the first being Copiousness, its fabulous wealth of words. The ground of our tongue is Old English, and as we have borrowed from the Briton, Roman, Dane, French, Italian and Spaniard, "how can our stock be other than exceeding plentiful?"

There have been attempts to write a language that rejects these borrowings, composed as far as possible of words of Old English origin, notably by William Morris towards the end of last century. At its best, as in *News from Nowhere*, this can be very moving in its simplicity, but when carried to extremes it is merely embarrassing. "There they abode a whole day, yet warily, since, though there were no waged men-at-arms in the stead, there went about many stout carles, who all bore long whittles, and looked as if their bills and bows had not been far to seek. But no strife betid." This is sham medievalism, as false as the imitation-antique furniture that used to be made in Wardour Street, after which this sort of writing is named: Wardour-Street English. And even though *waged, stout, strife* are so used as to give the impression of Old English words, they are all borrowings from Old French.

To write with an over-latinized vocabulary is equally false, but there is no reason why we should impoverish ourselves by rejecting our accumulated riches; indeed, there is every reason why we should make use of them, for its store of words is one of the glories of our language: a wealth of synonyms and near-synonyms that can impart the subtlest distinctions of meaning. Consider the words in a sentence taken at random from an essay by Johnson: "Knowledge is praised and desired by multitudes whom her charms could never rouse from the couch of sloth." *Knowledge*—wisdom, science, information; *praised*—applauded, lauded, commended, acclaimed, extolled, eulogised, glorified; *desired*—wanted, wished for, coveted; *multitude*—crowd, throng, horde; *charm*—attraction, enchantment, fascination, allurement; *rouse*—wake, stir, start; *couch*—

bed, sofa, ottoman, divan, mattress (the last four words are oriental); *sloth*—indolence, laziness, sluggishness, idleness, slackness. Merely by varying these words, Johnson could have written this simple sentence in a hundred different ways, with as many different shades of meaning. No other language has such a wealth of words, and this copiousness of the English vocabulary is an excellency comparable to the easiness of its grammar.

Finally, like Lear turning to Cordelia, "Now, our joy, although the last, not least," Carew turns to "the last and sweetest point of the sweetness of our tongue". But first he considers the merits and demerits of its competitors. Italian is pleasant, but without sinews; French delicate, "but even nice* as a woman, scarce daring to open her lips for fear of marring her countenance"; Spanish majestical, but "running too much on the O"; German manlike, but very harsh. In borrowing from them, however, English has selected their virtues and rejected their faults, giving "the strength of consonants to the Italian, the full sound of words to the French, the variety of terminations to the Spanish, and the mollifying of more vowels to the German". Like bees, we have gathered the honey of their good properties, so "how can the language which consisteth of all these sound other than most full of sweetness?"

If we make allowance for the patriotic fervour of an Elizabethan, there is much truth in this. English is a gentle language, its long contact with French during the Middle Ages having reduced the harshness of its Teutonic gutturals, so that in speech as well as in vocabulary it is a modification both of German and French, a forcible tongue, yet gentle as its climate and its landscape. Again, if German is over-stocked with consonants (*macht dich nicht*) and Italian with vowels (*Sola rossegia, e semplice la rosa*), English is a happy compromise between the two: to the strength of its consonantal Teutonic base adding the vocal music of Latin and Romance languages. And if Spanish lacks variety of terminations, in nothing is

---

* *Nice*, like so many adjectives, has had a variety of meanings. A Middle English borrowing from Old French *nice*, Latin *nescius*, ignorant, originally meant *foolish*, but Shakespeare used it in the sense of *fastidious, scrupulous, dainty, effeminate, insignificant, affected*, which last seems to be Carew's meaning.

English more remarkable than in its diversity of word-endings, of, indeed, its sounds as a whole. Although it may be criticized for its lack of rhymes, as the natural medium of blank verse, it cannot be charged with monotony. In the Johnson extract quoted above, no two word-endings are the same, nor are any of its syllables.

The vagaries of English spelling reflect the variety of its sounds. In addition to the consonants of the alphabet, there are the combinations: *ch* (church), *dg* (judge), *th* (the, thin), *ng* (singer, finger), *sh* (ship), *zh* (vision). And in addition to the five short and five long vowels, from *flat* to *flute*, there are more than as many other vowel sounds, from *part* to *put*. Then, to the variety of Old English and French-Latin words we add that of their prefixes and suffixes: *fore*-head, *pre*-fix; *un*-do, *dis-en*-tangle (a Scandinavian verb with two Latin-French prefixes); false-*hood*, decept-*ion*; friend-*ship*, ami-*ty*, and so on.*

Because two or more of the innumerable sounds and syllables in English rarely come together by accident (as here, *or more*), much of the beauty of its prose and verse lies in their unobtrusive assembly and repetition with variations, like a theme in music. As R. L. Stevenson wrote, playing on the labials *p*, *b*, *f*, *v*, *m*, liquid *l*, and *e*, *i*, *ow* vowels:

> The vowel demands to be repeated; the consonant demands to be repeated; and both cry aloud to be perpetually varied. You may follow the adventures of a letter through any passage that has particularly pleased you; find it, perhaps, denied a while, to tantalise the ear; find it fired again at you in a whole broadside; or find it pass into congenerous sounds, one liquid or labial melting away into another.

Then, according to Carew, comes the final excellency of the English tongue, the range and variety of its music. "The long words that we borrow, being intermingled with the short of our own store, make up a perfect harmony, by culling from out which mixture (with judgement) you may frame your speech according to the matter you must work on: majestical, pleasant, delicate or manly, more or less, in what sort you please." In other words, the English tongue has the full range of a

* See pp. 58, 77.

symphony orchestra: from the plucked and percussive consonantal music of the north to the long vowelled harmonies of
the Mediterranean; from Wyatt's

> Forget not yet the tried intent
> Of such a truth as I have meant;
> My great travail so gladly spent,
> Forget not yet!

to Tennyson's

> The Lotos blooms below the barren peak:
> The Lotos blows by every winding creek:
> All day the wind breathes low with mellower tone:
> Thro' every hollow cave and alley lone
> Round and round the spicy downs the yellow Lotos-
> dust is blown.

And here, perhaps, are the extremes of English prose style,
both sentences written at about the same time, soon after the
middle of the seventeenth century, the first by Bunyan, the
second by Sir Thomas Browne:

> As I walked through the wilderness of this world I lighted on
> a certain place where was a den, and laid me down in that
> place to sleep; and, as I slept, I dreamed a dream.

> But man is a noble animal, splendid in ashes, and pompous
> in the grave, solemnising nativities and deaths with equal
> lustre, nor omitting ceremonies of bravery in the infamy of
> his nature.

In the *Pilgrim's Progress* quotation, all but three of the words
are monosyllables, and all but two (certain place) are Old
English. Nothing could be simpler (though the play, probably
unconscious, on the related consonants *w-p*, *l-d* should be
noted): a succession of short words unadorned by adjectives
and, because virtually monosyllabic, dependent for its rhythm
on the phrase, and almost devoid of a subsidiary verbal
measure. If we read the passage aloud, the stressed words

are: walked through—wilderness—world—lighted—certain place—where—den—laid—down—that place—sleep—slept—dreamed—dream: fourteen English to three French-Latin words.

The second quotation, from *Urn Burial*, is worth more detailed analysis:

But		and
man		deaths
is		with
a		equal
	noble	lustre,
	animal,	nor
	splendid	omitting
in		ceremonies
ashes,		of
and		bravery
	pompous	in
in		the
the		infamy
grave,		of
	solemnising	his
	nativities	nature.

The nineteen words in the first column are Old English, all but one are monosyllables, and all but four colourless working-parts of speech. Contrasted with these are the words of two to four syllables, all of French and Latin origin: seven nouns, four adjectives and two verbs, and as all these words are stressed, the Latin element is overwhelming. It is a prose of sonorous vowels, with a verbal rhythm—"noble animal—solemnising nativities—omitting ceremonies"—which determines that of the whole. But the force of the four short English nouns should be observed, three of them concrete, contrasting with the six Latin abstractions. *Man* is the first, and essential word, the subject of the whole passage; *ashes* and *grave* are both heavily stressed as the culmination of their phrases, and how much more forcible is the pairing of *nativities* with *deaths* instead of, say, with the Latin *dissolutions*. In Bunyan the proportion of stressed English to stressed Latin words is fourteen to three, in

Browne it is reversed, four to thirteen. But neither passage would have meaning without the humble, indispensable English particles that hold it together, like the almost invisible chain along which pearls are strung.

"The long words that we borrow, being intermingled with the short of our own store, make up a perfect harmony." Carew did not live to read the works of Sir Thomas Browne, though he knew some of those of an even greater writer, his contemporary, Shakespeare. He cannot have read this, however, for *The Tempest* was not published in his lifetime. The text is that of the First Folio, 1623.

> Our Reuels now are ended: These our actors
> (As I foretold you) were all Spirits, and
> Are melted into Ayre, into thin Ayre;
> And, like the baseless fabricke of this vision,
> The Clowd-capt Towres, the gorgeous Pallaces,
> The solemne Temples, the great Globe it selfe,
> Yea, all which it inherit, shall dissolue,
> And, like this insubstantiall Pageant faded,
> Leaue not a racke behinde: we are such stuffe
> As dreames are made on; and our little life
> Is rounded with a sleepe.

Our		and,	leave
	revels	like	not
now		the	a
are		baseless	rack
ended:		fabric	behind:
these		of	we
our		this	are
	actors,	vision,	such
as		the	stuff
I		cloud-	as
foretold		capped	dreams
you,		towers,	are
were		the	made
all		gorgeous	on;
	spirits,	palaces,	and
and		the	our

```
are                         solemn       little
melted                      temples,     life
into             the                     is
        air,    great                            rounded
into                        globe        with
thin            itself,                  a
        air;    yea,                     sleep.
                all
                which
                it
                        inherit,
                shall
                        dissolve,
                and,
                like
                this
                        insubstantial
                        pageant
                        faded,
```

Two-thirds of the words in these lines, which must be among the noblest ever written, are of Old English origin, mostly unobtrusive monosyllables, though a dozen of them are charged with the profoundest meanings and associations, from *ended* to *sleep*. It is worth noting that *rack*, a Middle English word of Scandinavian origin, meaning wind-driven clouds of the upper air, is first used here in the figurative sense of trace.

Most of the French-Latin words were borrowed during the Middle English period, but *cap, tower, temple* were among the first to be taken direct from Latin into Old English. It is some measure of Shakespeare's importance as a maker of modern English that this is the first use of the adjectives *baseless* and *insubstantial*, and of *rounded* in the sense of come full circle, completed.

Here, indeed, are the excellencies of copiousness and sweetness that constitute a delight. An air of insubstantiality is imparted to the three introductory lines of mainly English words by the large proportion, more than a half, that begin with a vowel and fade to the ethereal fragility of "into air, into thin air". The next five lines of Latin polysyllables rise to the worldly crescendo of "gorgeous palaces" before sinking again into the quiet, falling cadence of "insubstantial pageant faded"; and with *faded* the pageantry dissolves into three lines of native monosyllables, unified by the simple sequence, *leave, dreams, sleep*. And throughout runs the harmonizing disyllabic counterpoint that opposes the rising rhythm of the metre: *revels, ended, melted*, linked by *faded* to the series of labials and stressed *a*'s: *baseless, fabric, palaces, pageant*, before closing in "*rounded* with a sleep".

And thus, if mine own eyes be not blinded by affection, I have made yours to see that the most renowned of other nations have laid up, as in treasure, and entrusted the *divisos orbe Britannos* [remote Britons] with the rarest jewels of their lips' perfections, whether you respect the understanding for significancy, or the memory for easiness, or the conceit for plentifulness, or the ear for pleasantness.

FUTURE ENGLISH

So LONG AS a language is spoken it is a living thing, and like all forms of life is subject to change. Old English can have borne little resemblance to the Indo-European tongue from which it was descended, and Modern English bears little apparent resemblance to Old English. Only in the seventh century did English become a written language, and the prose of 970, a thousand years ago, means little to the ordinary reader today: "Men þa leofostan, geþenceaþ þæt ge gelomlice winnað, and a embe þæt sorgiað þæt we ure lichoman gefyllan and gefrætwiað." But five hundred years later it had become very different, as Caxton ruefully wrote, and printed, in 1470: "And also my lorde abbot of westmynster ded do shewe to me late certayn euydences [documents] wryton in olde englysshe for to reduce it in to our englysshe now usid. And certaynly it was wreton in suche wyse that it was more lyke to dutche [German] than englysshe I coude not reduce ne brynge it to be vnderstonden." That is not Modern English, but it is much closer to the English of 500 years later than to the Old English of 500 years before.

The dissemination of books was the main reason why change became slower after the Middle Ages, for the printed word tends to preserve; it is the spoken word that leads to change. Then, the standardization of spelling by about 1650, and Johnson's Dictionary of a hundred years later made for greater stability of pronunciation and usage. But by this time there were almost as many English-speakers in America as there were in Britain, separated by weeks of perilous sailing, and almost as much out of contact with one another as had been the Aryans of Scandinavia with those of the Mediterranean.

English is a language peculiarly susceptible to change of pronunciation. First, because of its range of vowels and diphthongs, which are altered by a slight change in the position of the tongue. Then, because there is no rule governing the position of the stress in a word: *pórtrait, portráy; necéssity, nécessary; conservátion, consérvative*; and standard *fórmidable* (French *formidáble*) is fast becoming BBC *formídable*. So, while the English began to broaden the *a* of some words (*path—parth*), though the *r* was not pronounced, and to abbreviate some long words, reducing the stress on later syllables (*témp'rary, térrit'ry*), the Americans retained the flat *a*, and pronunciation of more vowels (*temp80áiry, territóry*), though consonants sometimes disappeared, like the *t* in *city*. Then, American pronunciation became more nasal, flatter (fla"er), less lively and varied than English, probably as a result of other European immigrants haltingly learning the language.

For the Victorians, American English was only a joke. "Thou callest trousers *pants*, whereas I call them *trousers*," Samuel Butler wrote satirically. It is true that *trousers* (Celtic *trius*) is centuries older than the American slang for *pantaloons*, but American *suspenders* appears to be slightly older than English *braces*, and the Victorians borrowed the word to describe the contraption that held up their stockings and socks.

It was not long before the English had to take the American language very seriously. When the United States entered the Great War in 1917 it emerged from three centuries of isolation, and for the first time Americans in their thousands landed in Britain. Until this time the influence of America on the English language had been virtually confined to books, but now came the spoken word, intensified by the invention of wireless, or what the Americans called radio and, a few years later, of the talkie, the talking film. The influence was still further intensified by the Second World War, the development of air travel that followed it, and the invention of television, which brought American speech into almost every English home; and not only English, but also into the homes of millions of people all over the world who speak the language, or partially understand it. Not so very long ago, speech travelled by land or water at the speed of horse or sailing-ship, and audiences were confined to hundreds; but today it travels by air at the speed of light, and can be heard by all the men in the world and the man in the moon. Never before has the influence of the spoken word been anything like as powerful as it is today; and it is the spoken word that makes for change.

The English carried "the treasure of our tongue" to America, and later to the Antipodes, to Australia and New Zealand, to India, Africa and all the other places that made up the second British Empire. The Empire has gone, but English remains: English of a sort; for the students of northern Nigeria can barely understand the English of their Indian teachers, and the English of the various Indian states is diverging into dialects so different that their speakers cannot understand one another. This is inevitable; English cannot be expected to survive in any purity as a second language among peoples with a very different language of their own and a quite different cultural heritage. But even where it is the native language, American rather than English is becoming the standard: in Canada, of course, but also in Australia.

For there are now two standards, and it may be that the tongue spoken by 200 million Americans will prevail over that spoken by less than a third of that number in Britain, that "when two-thirds of the people who use a certain language decide to call it a *freight-train* instead of a *goods-train* they are 'right', and the first is correct English and the second a dialect." Or perhaps it will end in compromise. If greater numbers and wealth, and a continuous bombardment of inter-continental ballistic vocables reduce the English into acceptance of American pronunciation and vocabulary—*freight-train* for *goods-train*, *elevator* for *lift*, *gas* for *petrol*, *faucet* for *tap*, even the dreadful *mortician* for *undertaker*—it may be that in return Americans will enliven the monotony of their speech with the greater variety of English intonation.

But even if the two become one standard speech, there will still be change, unless English ceases to be spoken and, like Latin, becomes a dead language, frozen and embalmed. That is improbable within the foreseeable future, and the important thing is to prevent change degenerating into corruption. It will not be easy in this new era of the spoken word. There is the constant threat of jargon, the esoteric terminology of a science or profession; of verbiage, long meaningless words that obscure rather than illuminate; of sheer vulgarity and philistinism; of the exploiters, for whom language is merely a salesman's device for raucous propaganda, or the enticing subliminal whisperings of advertisement. Under these pressures, English is already losing its dominant position as a cultural medium, and becoming the utilitarian language of business and "good jobs". Pidgin is the Chinese corruption of business, and pidgin English is the international jargon of commerce.

The population of China is much the biggest in the world, some 800 million, its cultural history far longer than that of Europe and America, and it may be that one day Chinese will be the international language. Not until it is unified and simplified, however, for its speech is divided and sub-divided into numerous dialects, and its writing too difficult for anybody but specialist scholars to learn. Meanwhile English, so easy to learn, and the native speech of some 300 million people, twice as many as those who speak Spanish or Russian, is likely to remain the principal language of the world. There have been attempts to propagate manufactured languages, of which Volapuk (World-speech) is the first, and Esperanto (Hoping-one) the best known, but they have not flourished. A language is a living thing, sprung from the mouths of men and women, an organic growth like a flower or tree that draws life and sustenance through its roots in the soil where it was planted. It will bear transplantation into a not too alien ground; but a manufactured language is an artificial flower pushed into sand, rootless, lifeless, incapable of growth, and doomed to decay. And a language without a literature is not worth learning.

Language serves two purposes. The first and fundamental one, for it was its engendering, is utilitarian: a means of communication between people, of exchanging greetings, information, ideas, of forwarding the ordinary business of life. For such a purpose, precision of meaning, what Carew called "significancy", is essential; but for its second purpose, which is to delight, imprecision is equally important. Words have a beauty of their own, and with age accumulate associations more and more remote, so that a simple word like *road* or *silent* has a thousand connotations. And a sequence of words rhythmically and harmoniously arranged, whether in prose or verse, conveys, like music, meanings beyond the range of definition. A language is nourished and sustained by its literature, and without a living literature it will wither.

Among languages, as among all other living things, there is a constant, unconscious struggle for survival, and the language with the greatest number of advantages at a given moment of time will become pre-eminent. To its other main advantages of wide dispersal, ease of learning, and copious vocabulary, the English language has an incomparable literature, and it seems probable that the tongue will continue to spread for as long as we can see into the future. But the English we know is barely six centuries old, and language itself only as old as man, about a million years, and man, if he does not destroy himself, has a life of some 50,000 million years before him. What language will be like even in a minute fraction of that time, another million years, is past the size of dreaming, though we may be sure that, like the insubstantial pageant of *The Tempest*, the English language will long have faded, though leaving, perhaps, the wraith of a rack behind.

BIBLIOGRAPHY
AND INDEX

A BRIEF BIBLIOGRAPHY

The following books, to many of which I am myself indebted, should prove useful and interesting to those who wish to pursue further the story of language and the English tongue:

BAUGH, A. C. *A History of the English Language*, Routledge, London, 1951.

BOLTON, W. F., ed. *The English Language*, Vol. I: *Essays by English and American Men of Letters 1490–1839*, Cambridge University Press, 1966.

BOLTON, W. F. & CRYSTAL, D., eds. *The English Language*, Vol. 2: *Essays by Linguists and Men of Letters 1858–1964*, Cambridge University Press, 1969.

BRADLEY, H. *The Making of English*, Macmillan, London, 1920.

BROOK, G. L. *An Introduction to Old English*, Manchester University Press, 1955.

BURGESS, A. *Language Made Plain*, English Universities Press, London, 1964.

CLARK, J. W. *Early English: A Study of Old and Middle English*, Deutsch, London, 1957.

DIRINGER, D. *Writing*, Thames & Hudson, London, 1962.

MENCKEN, H. L. *The American Language*, Routledge, London, 1936.

PARTRIDGE, E. H. *A Dictionary of Slang*, Routledge, London, 1936.

PICKLES, C. & MEYNELL, L. *The Beginning of Words*, Blond, London, 1970.

POTTER, S. *Our Language*, Penguin, London, 1969.

WEEKLEY, E. *The Romance of Words*, Murray, London, 1912–1961.

In a lighter vein there are:

BROWN, I., his "Word Books" from *A Word in Your Ear*, 1942, to *Words in Season*, Hart-Davis, London, 1961.

HERBERT, A. P. *What a Word!*, Methuen, London, 1935.

Bibliography

Valuable recordings of Chaucer's English have recently been made:

The Prologue to the Canterbury Tales and *The Nun's Priest's Tale*, read in Middle English by N. Coghill, N. Davis, and J. Burrow, 1964, 1966. Argo Record Co. RG 401, 466.

INDEX

Compiled by H. E. CROWE

123

Index

Normans, effect on language, 66–9
  invasion of, 83
Norse invaders, 60, 61, 63, 83, 96
  language, 62
North Teutons, 60
Northumbria, 44, 54, 56, 65, 68
  conquered by Danes, 60
  converted, 55
  culture, 55, 64
  dialect, 54
Norway, 60
Norwegian language, 46, 65
Nouns, 100

Ogham alphabet, 42, 51
Ogma, inventor of alphabet, 42
Old English language, 44–53, 64, 69,
  75, 87, 95, 97, 106, 109, 110, 112,
  114
  grammar, 68
  Latin words in, 58, 59
  pronunciation, 52
Old French words in English, 87, 106
Old High German language, 46, 50
Old Low German, 46
Old Norse, 64
Old Stone Age, artists of, 23
Onomatopoeic word, 31, 34
Origin of Species, The (Darwin), 21
Orkneys, 40
Oxford, Earl of, 101
Oxford English Dictionary, 94, 95, 96–7

Painting, new words from, 89
Palate in speech, 24, 25, 29
Palestine, 37
Paper, invention of, 34
Papyrus, 34, 35
Paradise Lost (Milton), 88
Partridge, Eric, 95
Pastoral Care (Pope Gregory), King
  Alfred's version, 57, 69
Patrick, St, converts Ireland, 54
Persian language, 45
Peterborough, 69
Phoenicians, alphabet of, 38
Phoneme, 94
Phonetics, 94
Pictograms, 35, 36, 37
Pidgin English, 117
Pierce Penilesse (Nashe), 81
Pilgrim Fathers, 87
Pilgrim's Progress (Bunyan), 109
Place-names, 48, 63
Plymouth, Massachusetts, 87
Polish language, 45
Political terms, 62
Polychronicon (Higden), 71, 72, 77
Pope, Alexander, 89, 90
Pope Gregory, 57

Portuguese language, effect on vocabulary, 45, 89
Possessive case, 104
Prayer Book, sixteenth century, 52
Prepositions, 86, 103
Present tense, 90
Printing, influence on English language,
  79, 80–3
Progress of the Soul, The (Donne), 102
Pronunciation, 28, 29, 83, 98, 99–100,
  114–15
  American, 116
  Caxton and, 82
  foreigners and, 105
  invasions, effect of, 65
  variations, 27
Puberty, effect of on voice, 24
Purists and new words, 89
Puritan emigrants, 87

Radio, effect of, 115
Reformation, 84
Religion, 80
  Christianity becomes official, 43
*Remaines of a greater work concerning
  Britaine* (Camden), 17
Renaissance, 80, 84
Restoration, French influence on, 89
Robert of Gloucester, quoted, 70–1
Roman/Romans, 44, 47, 66, 67, 94
  alphabet, 38–9, 55, 61, 82, 99
  Christianity in Britain, 51
  civilization of Britain, 51
  Conquest, 41
  Empire, 43
  fortresses, 41, 42, 43
  names, 48
  roads, 42
Romance languages, 45, 66, 67
"Ruin, The", poem, 55
Russian language, 45, 117

St Albans, 13, 42
Sanskrit language, 45, 46
Saxonia, 44
Saxons, in Britain, 43, 44, 54
  words of, 63
Scandinavians, 78, 112
  invasions, effect on language, 56, 60,
  61, 62, 63
  place-names, 63, 64
  surnames, 63
  terminations, 63
Science and new words, 89, 93, 94
Scotland, 42, 44
  Celts in, 40–1
Second World War, 115
Semantics, 94
Semitic alphabet and language, 37–8,
  41

127